THE PRISON LETTERS

MATT MCCHLERY

kevin
mayhew

First Published in 2022 by Kevin Mayhew Ltd,

Fengate Farm,

Rattlesden,

Bury St Edmunds,

Suffolk, IP30 0SZ

Copyright © 2022 by Matt McChlery

ISBN (paperback): 9781838581350

ISBN (eBook): 9781838581367

Paperback product code: 1501710

eBook product code: 1501711

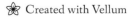 Created with Vellum

For Mike
a great mentor and friend

CONTENTS

PRAISE FOR MATT MCCHLERY

What others are saying about this book:

I know that devotional books are not supposed to be binge read but when I started reading Matt McChlery's book I found I couldn't put it down. That's not to say that it wouldn't have impacted me even more if I had paced myself. It was just that I found it really inspiring and accessible. Matt's selection of bible verses are so spot on and his illustrations are all so relevant, I wondered if he could keep it up for 40 days. Well, he certainly does and I wholeheartedly recommend it as a Lent devotional. It is challenging as well as informative and well worth reading all over again - this time allowing for the intended one-day-at-a-time reflections. Thank you Matt. It is really incredibly helpful as well as a good read, and I trust that for many it will be truly life-changing. I am already thinking about who I can give a copy to.

- Dr Hugh Osgood
    Founding President, Churches in Communities International and Past-President, Churches Together in England

In his introduction, author Matt McChlery invites the reader to rip open the envelopes containing Paul's prison letters and start reading. When I did so, I found the Bible passages brought alive with illustrations from Matt's family and church life, his childhood memories, sport, nature and even a pair of old walking boots. The topics he brings out from the letters are easy to relate to and I could easily imagine Paul writing these same things to our churches today. This Lent course is ideal for new and established Christians alike to delve into Biblical truths at any time of the year.

- Jane Walters
     Author and Retreat Leader

I first met Matt well over twenty years ago and was impressed with his zeal and dedication. And that devotion has only grown through years of service, faithfulness, and many challenges. And now he offers us time-tested wisdom worked out in the anvil of everyday life.

   I am sure you will be strengthened as you meditate on this devotional. Matt's self-depreciating candour and down-to-earth style make it easily relatable. It has compact and digestible daily readings that are biblical, practical, and encouraging. And prayers and questions that will take you deeper and further.

   Be blessed as you draw near to our beautiful and magnificent Lord and Saviour Jesus Christ, who is crucified, resurrected, and enthroned in glory. He is worthy of it all!

- Gareth Lowe
     Pastor, Every Nation Berlin

What a great idea! Journeying through Lent with the prison letters of the Apostle Paul and along key themes in the life of the follower of Jesus. These devotionals look at how the life, death and resurrection of Jesus Christ practically impacts the journey of the believer. Each day starts with a verse that underpins the focus for the day, along with a personal anecdote that often highlights Matt's own depth of relationship with Jesus and culminates in a short prayer. This devotional can also be used in a group setting with discussion questions along all the key themes and wider reading that highlights an important message written by Paul while in chains, when he would have weighed every word carefully, and allowing the reader an opportunity to go deeper in their walk with Christ. I love it!

- Ruth O'Reilly-Smith
    Writer and Broadcaster

Matt McChlery writes with infectious enthusiasm and passion as he works thematically through the subjects that most concerned Paul during his imprisonment. I love the concept of gathering all of Paul's prison letters, reading them with that unique context in mind; and Matt leads us through them with wisdom, humour and insight, bringing a new light to familiar passages.

- Amy Scott Robinson
    Author and Editor

INTRODUCTION

I love receiving handwritten letters. I don't know if it is because of the increasingly digital world we live in or the fact that as I write this, my email inbox currently has 999+ unread emails sitting in it. A handwritten letter captures my attention. I can see that the sender has taken time and effort to communicate something with me and it is all the more meaningful and personal because of it.

This collection of letters: Ephesians, Philippians, Colossians and Philemon, were written by Paul whilst he was imprisoned and being held under house arrest in Rome. Paul finds himself in a serious situation and acknowledges that the end result of this imprisonment might end with his execution (Philippians 1:20). Knowing this makes me sit up and listen a bit more keenly to what is being said as I believe Paul would be wanting to communicate the most important instruction and teaching, especially sensing it could be his last.

These letters are sometimes addressed to specific churches such as Philippians which was written to 'all the saints in Christ Jesus' (Philippians 1:1) at a church in a place called Philippi, which you can find in modern day Greece. Here, as in many other places in this translation of the Bible, the word 'saints' simply means 'God's people'.

Whereas some of the letters are for specific individuals such as Philemon that was addressed to 'Philemon our dear friend and co-worker, to Apphia our sister, to Archippus our fellow-soldier, and to the church in your house' (Philemon 1-2).

I have not unpacked every verse of the four books – that would be a much longer study! Rather, I have identified some of the main themes that run through them that lend themselves to a lent devotional and have drawn them together in chapters. However, reading each book in its entirety to help provide context to those verses that have been selected is highly recommended.

Some may well be wondering what Lent is about, as it is observed in some, but not all, traditions of Christianity. Lent is a period in the church calendar year consisting of forty days which lead up to Easter Sunday (not including Sundays). During this time, we remember and reflect upon Jesus' time of fasting and temptation in the wilderness just after his baptism – which is why many people who observe Lent also choose to fast something during the forty days. Fasting is when something is given up for a time. It can be food, or something we particularly enjoy like chocolate or watching TV. Fasting is a spiritual discipline and helps us to grow in our discipleship as all spiritual disciplines do.

The themes of family and unity can be seen in the Lenten narrative at Jesus' baptism shortly before he departs into the wilderness for forty days where we see the three persons of the Trinity present interacting and relating to each other (Matthew 3:16-17). Whilst in the wilderness Jesus was fasting (Luke 4:1-2) and praying. Near the end of this time, we also see Jesus engaging in spiritual warfare as he resists Satan's temptations (Luke 4:3-13). During this experience, as well as in the events that led up to Jesus' crucifixion, He suffered. He died on the cross and then rose again on Easter Sunday which has eternal implications.

Indeed, these prison letters contain some amazing insights into what it means to live a life of discipleship in a vibrant relationship with Jesus. The best part is that these letters are not stuck in a time capsule – they contain spiritual insight that is still alive and relevant to our lives today.

So, as we start this 40-day journey together, tear open the envelopes and carefully unfold the pages of these amazing letters, let us ask the Holy Spirit to come and enliven God's Word to us and to show us how to live for Jesus today.

HOW TO USE THIS BOOK

This book was primarily written as a Lent devotional, which is why the first Chapter has a smaller number of entries than the rest – beginning on Ash Wednesday does not give a whole week. This is also the reason why Jesus's death and resurrection are saved until the final chapter.

Each chapter has a devotional for each day of the week except Sunday, as traditionally Lent is not observed on Sundays.

The end of each chapter also includes a reading plan to help you read through all the prison letters in their entirety. There are also some suggestions for wider Bible reading on the theme for that week as well as some discussion questions that could be used within a small group or for personal reflection.

Although designed with Lent in mind, this book does not have to be strictly confined to Lent – it can be read at any time of year

PART I

FAMILY

DAY 1 - ADOPTION

Blessed be the God and Father of our Lord Jesus Christ, who has blessed us in Christ with every spiritual blessing in the heavenly places, just as he chose us in Christ before the foundation of the world to be holy and blameless before him in love. He destined us for adoption as his children through Jesus Christ, according to the good pleasure of his will, to the praise of his glorious grace that he freely bestowed on us in the Beloved. (Ephesians 1:3-6)

Adopting someone is a big step to take, yet it is also profoundly beautiful and powerful. It is also a very invasive and rigorous process.

I have a friend in my church who adopted her daughter some years ago. She endured a six-month process where social workers quizzed, probed, and investigated every area of her life in order to check that she would be able to care for her daughter adequately. Then came the meetings between her and her daughter for them to get to know each other a bit before she came to live with her permanently.

Even after her daughter had moved in, there was still a

probationary period that lasted a year where the adoption process could be halted if necessary.

So, after many hurdles, it was with great joy and celebration when I, along with a bunch of other friends and family, squeezed into the family courtroom at Norwich Crown Court to witness the adoption of her daughter into her family.

We celebrated magnificently afterwards.

Adoption is a good image to use to help us understand what happens when we decide to follow Jesus. We are adopted into His family. God becomes our Father and other Christians, who are also adopted into this same family, are our brothers and sisters.

Have you heard the old joke - You can choose your friends, but you can't choose your family? Well, that doesn't really apply when it comes to adoption. Both the parents and the child get to choose – and the same is true for us because we get to choose to follow Jesus or not.

When we do choose Jesus, our life is completely made new in the spirit. We give up our dead spirit and exchange it for a new, living spirit. Empowered by this new spirit, we put aside our old way of life and take up a new way of life. One where Jesus is in charge, where we live to love and obey His leading. We seek to do His will and lay aside our own.

Yes, it is a life of sacrifice, but there are many benefits too. When we are adopted into God's family, we carry the family name of God – Christian. We are empowered to live a rejuvenated supernatural life by the indwelling of the Holy Spirit and this in turn helps us to make positive and lasting change upon the lives we encounter in the world around us. And yes, we are also promised eternal life where we will be together with Jesus and live in His presence forever with the absence of sin, death, and pain.

As we begin this 40-day journey together, there may be things in our lives that we have held on to from the days before our adoption into God's family. Or there may be choices and behaviours that we have made recently that are not in line with the will of God.

Ash Wednesday marks the beginning of Lent and is an

opportunity for us to repent and confess our sin. Repentance is more than saying 'sorry'. It is a deliberate turning away. We choose to turn away from our sin and walk in the direction and will of Jesus instead. There is a change that takes place, a change that is only possible with the empowering help of the Holy Spirit and our complete reliance upon Him.

This may be something we need to do today, whether it is Ash Wednesday or not. Repentance is not tied to a specific day or event.

Turn to Jesus today, right now wherever you are. Today is the day of repentance.

Jesus, I come to you today knowing that I have failed to live my life in the way you want me to live it. I am sorry for the way I have been living and for the things I continue to think and do that are against your will. Please forgive me. Today I choose to repent, to turn away from these things and to allow your Holy Spirit to work inside me to help me to follow you. Help me to live as your adopted child. I can't do it without you, Jesus.
Amen.

DAY 2 – FROM SLAVE TO BROTHER

I am sending him, that is, my own heart, back to you. I wanted to keep him with me, so that he might be of service to me in your place during my imprisonment for the gospel; but I preferred to do nothing without your consent, in order that your good deed might be voluntary and not something forced. Perhaps this is the reason he was separated from you for a while, so that you might have him back for ever, no longer as a slave but as more than a slave, a beloved brother—especially to me but how much more to you, both in the flesh and in the Lord. (Philemon 12-16)

These verses are taken from the very short letter Paul wrote to Philemon about one of Philemon's slaves, Onesimus.

For a reason we are not told, Onesimus has gone away from his master and has sought out Paul in prison. One thing we do know is that whilst he was with Paul, he became a Christian.

Paul now sends him back to Philemon with a glowing endorsement and appeals to him to welcome his former slave back and to forgive him for whatever he has done.

However, Paul goes one step further than just appealing for reconciliation and forgiveness. Knowing that when someone becomes a Christian they are adopted into the family of Christ, that their spiritual status has changed and that fellow Christians are now brothers and sisters, Paul appeals to Philemon to accept Onesimus not as a slave, but as a brother.

This letter shows us that our faith in Jesus breaks down any social barriers that may exist[1].

I was brought up in Zimbabwe, a landlocked country in southern Africa. When I was born, the country was just emerging from a civil war that divided the nation along racial lines. Growing up, I was aware of racial tensions nevertheless, especially since becoming a Christian in my early teens, I found that in Christ I had many brothers and sisters with whom I shared strong friendships despite race or gender.

Now living in Wisbech, in the north-east of Cambridgeshire in the UK, there is a big immigrant community in the town mainly due to the factories and farming industries that are here. Again, language barriers have made it difficult for churches to reach out. Recently a Bulgarian family has started coming to our church and every day we are finding a common bond and purpose that exists between us because of our relationship with Jesus, despite the language difficulties.

Social barriers are many and varied and can be based on a wide variety of things. But the letter Paul wrote to Philemon shows us that all of these can be overcome by the grace and love of Jesus at work within us.

This causes me to pause and ask myself if my relationships with others are being hindered by any social barriers – whether they are a Christian or not. Do I avoid a certain type of person because engaging with them would just be hard work? Do I neglect nurturing relationships with people who may take more than they give to the relationship? Am I worried by what others may think of me if I am friends with a certain person or group of people? Do I *really* accept that fellow Christians are actually my brothers and sisters despite their background or ethnic heritage, and do I behave in ways that reflect this belief?

These questions are challenging, but they are important.

If we were in the position that Philemon found himself in, would we forgive the former slave for whatever it was he had done to cause him to run away? Would we accept him back because a Christian leader whom we respect has asked us to do so? And would we take things that extra step further and accept and treat Onesimus no longer as a slave, but welcome him in as part of our family?

Maybe there is someone in your life who has been brought to mind as you have read this devotional today whom you don't particularly get along with, or don't see them as being a 'brother' or 'sister' in Christ despite the fact they are a Christian? Can I encourage you to pray for them, and for yourself? Ask Jesus to show you what it means to live and love as part of his global family.

Jesus, help me to love my Christian brothers and sisters as you want me to love them. Help me to overcome any social barriers that may exist – knowing that your love breaks these barriers down and brings us together. Lord, give me your grace and patience. Help me to recognise those around me who are on the edge of faith, to draw them closer to you by showing them what it means to be a member of your family.
Amen.

DAY 3 – WE ARE THE BODY OF CHRIST

But speaking the truth in love, we must grow up in every way into him who is the head, into Christ, from whom the whole body, joined and knitted together by every ligament with which it is equipped, as each part is working properly, promotes the body's growth in building itself up in love. (Ephesians 4:15-16)

I enjoy watching detective programmes on the TV. Every so often the detective needs to solve the case of a body that has been dismembered. Often a piece of crucial evidence is missing because the body is not whole, and the rest of the episode centres around how the detective team goes about locating this piece of evidence to ultimately reveal who the killer is – which they so often manage to do very neatly within the sixty-minute time frame.

In today's reading, Paul describes the Church as Jesus' body on the earth. Jesus is the head of the Church, and the body holds together and grows because of love and because each part of the body, although different in function and appearance, plays its part and does what God has called them to do.

Notice how the body is encouraged towards maturity by the truth being spoken in love. This means correction and guidance is given gently, yet uncompromisingly.

As people who believe in Jesus and have given control of our lives and destiny over to Him, we are part of God's family. We are adopted and accepted and loved by God our Father and we are also related to every single Christian on earth. Together we form His body, living out who Jesus is and showing His love through word and action to the hurting and broken world around us.

When I dropped a hammer onto my toe, my whole body was affected. The pain seemed overwhelming and caused me to cry out. It made me limp quickly towards the freezer to find something cold to put on it to help alleviate the agony and swelling. When part of the body is hurt, injured or suffering, it impacts the rest of the body regardless of how small or seemingly insignificant it is.

Going back to my detective TV programmes, one obvious thing to note about dismembered bodies is that they are dead! There is no life in them. Indeed, if we have no legs, we cannot walk, or if we have no eyes we cannot see. This may seem silly to point out – it's so obvious. But what about when it applies to church?

Are we recognising and encouraging all within the body of the church to carry out their God-given function? Are we allowing the eyes to see? Are we encouraging the ears to hear and the mouths to speak?

And when we zoom our view out a bit and look at the wider Church with all its diversity, are we working together to further the gospel or is the body dismembered and lifeless?

We are the Church. We are the hope on earth because we carry the awesome supernatural resurrection power of Jesus Christ within us and He commissions us to spread the Gospel to all the world – that Jesus is alive! That He loves them and invites them to join in His amazing family too. And one day we will all live together in a new heaven and a new earth with Jesus where His righteousness and kingdom shall rule forever.

We are better together. We were not called to walk this road of faith in Jesus alone. In fact, the opposite is true. We are actually called to live and work as a family and as a body, where we need to rely upon each other and are incomplete without each other.

Jesus, thank you for your Church. Thank you for my spiritual family. Help me to strengthen and encourage those within my church as we live together as your body. I ask that you increase the unity between individuals and churches, that we may work together to further your Kingdom in this place.
Amen.

DAY 4 - NO LONGER FOREIGNERS

So then you are no longer strangers and aliens, but you are citizens with the saints and also members of the household of God, built upon the foundation of the apostles and prophets, with Christ Jesus himself as the cornerstone. In him the whole structure is joined together and grows into a holy temple in the Lord; in whom you also are built together spiritually into a dwelling-place for God. (Ephesians 2:19-22)

When I first moved to the UK, things were very different and strange to me. The trees were dissimilar. The weather was certainly not what I was used to coming from Zimbabwe. The supermarkets were so big and contained so much choice! The money felt strange. There were a whole set of social norms I was unfamiliar with. The concept of 'wildlife' was unusual (in Zimbabwe bugs and ants are considered pests, not wildlife). The vocabulary was different too and I had to relearn the names of many everyday objects for me to be understood.

I was a foreigner in a foreign land.

It is very easy for someone unfamiliar with the language and culture of a country, or even of a church, to feel separate and alone.

However, Christians are not to shun or reject anyone.

Today's passage comes at the end of a longer section that speaks of Jew and Gentile being brought together and reconciled through Christ.

Historically, Jews and Gentiles did not mix. From their understanding of the Old Testament scriptures, the Jewish people quite correctly saw themselves as the covenant people of God, and therefore anyone who was not a Jew was outside of this agreement – a Gentile.

However, Jesus not only fulfils the Old Testament, He also brings a New Covenant that includes everyone. In Christ, there is no longer a separation between Jew and Gentile. Those who were outside the Old Covenant are now brought in and made fellow citizens of the Kingdom of God that Jesus was telling everyone about. Based upon the firm foundation, the cornerstone that is Jesus Himself.

Elsewhere in another letter Paul wrote to the Galatian church, this idea is extended further: "There is no longer Jew or Greek, there is no longer slave or free, there is no longer male and female; for all of you are one in Christ Jesus. And if you belong to Christ, then you are Abraham's offspring, heirs according to the promise." (Galatians 3:28-29).

This was revolutionary thinking at the time. The idea that Jews and Gentiles could work and live together was unheard of. Let alone suggesting that societal notions of what it means to be a man or a woman and their roles and place in society were not to be separate, with one more powerful than the other, but to co-exist as equals.

Paul is saying that in Christ, we are all equal. Our 'citizenship' of the Kingdom of God is the same as each other. Indeed, because we are in Christ, we are all part of the same family and all share in the same inheritance that God has promised His children.

In Jesus, the whole building of the Church – His family, His bride – is held together and rises to become a holy temple.

We are reminded that we too are being built together. We are each living stones (1 Peter 2:5) that are shaped and moulded by the working of the Holy Spirit. We help to form the structure of this thing called 'church'. We are part of His holy church, but more than this, we are part of the family of God.

Let's pause and allow the Holy Spirit to examine our hearts and ask Him to show us if there is anyone in our lives whom we may be treating unequally. Let us also ask for help to put things right.

Perhaps you may feel like a foreigner in the church or may know of someone who does? Let us ask the Holy Spirit to give us guidance and wisdom to help us integrate all those whom God has brought to us so they may feel they belong.

Jesus, thank you that we are part of your family. Please help us to treat others as equals. Show us those in our church who may be feeling left out or alone and show us how we can help them to feel they belong.
Amen.

FURTHER READING &
QUESTIONS 1

PHILEMON

Wider Reading – Family

Children of God - Galatians 3:26-4:7

The Prodigal Son - Luke 15:11-32

Unity and Diversity - 1 Corinthians 12:12-31

Love your Neighbour - James 2:8-9

How to treat Foreigners - Leviticus 19:33-34

No Favouritism - Acts 10:34-43

Discussion Questions - Family

In what ways does the story of the Prodigal Son mirror the situation with the runaway slave Onesimus we find in Philemon?

How are they alike / different?

What can we learn from this?

The church is described as 'the body of Christ'. What part of the body do you think you are? In other words - what gifts, skills or talents do you have to contribute to the church?

How could you use these gifts, skills and talents more in your context?

Have you ever been to a foreign country? How did it feel being a foreigner in a different place?

Is there anyone in your church who may be feeling like an outsider? What can you do to help them feel like they belong?

PART II

UNITY

DAY 5 – GOD'S PLAN

In him we have redemption through his blood, the forgiveness of our trespasses, according to the riches of his grace that he lavished on us. With all wisdom and insight he has made known to us the mystery of his will, according to his good pleasure that he set forth in Christ, as a plan for the fullness of time, to gather up all things in him, things in heaven and things on earth. (Ephesians 1:7-10)

I came across a website the other day that specialised in selling t-shirts that had common Zimbabwean expressions printed on them. Being brought up in Zimbabwe, this piqued my interest, and I went clicking through all the various phrases they had used on their clothing line. Many made me smile and some made me laugh out loud. One of the phrases used was 'make a plan'. In Zimbabwe, if something went wrong, or something unexpected happened, part of the resilience of its citizens was to not panic but to simply 'make a plan'.

The Zimbabwean version of 'making a plan' is quite re-actionary to ever changing circumstances and hardships. However, God's plans are quite deliberate and made well in advance.

I appreciate that there are a variety of different theological positions on atonement, and we may not agree on everything. However, I believe that here we see it is through Jesus' death on the cross that we are redeemed (released from slavery to sin and Satan because Jesus paid our ransom price) and forgiven because God chose to pour his grace upon us. God has revealed his salvation plan to us, His people, which was why Jesus came to us. The salvation Jesus offers is to restore and repair the broken relationship between us and God. But it is also to repair the brokenness of all creation[1].

It is in Jesus that true unity between people, God and creation can be restored. Jesus brings everything into a coherent whole and it is only through Jesus that the death, destruction and brokenness of humanity and creation can be made new once again.

Unity was God's idea.

Maybe this is why unity is so difficult to achieve.

There is great power in unity. We can achieve more together than we could ever achieve apart. If God intends to bring everything into complete unity and harmony in Christ, this puts it in the cross hairs of the enemy's sniper rifle as he seeks to kill, destroy and to move people away from God and His plans.

However, knowing that unity is part of the plans and purposes of God and is wrapped up in the redemption and salvation of Jesus, can encourage us to promote and strengthen the unity that exists between the people within our churches and, in a wider context, between different church groups.

We need to change our thinking and move away from 'my church' and 'your church'. Instead, we need to work towards the more unified understanding that Paul had.

When writing these letters, he addressed them to 'To all the saints in Christ Jesus who are in Philippi' (Philippians 1:1) or 'To the saints and faithful brothers and sisters in Christ in Colossae' (Colossians 1:2). He addressed them to believers within a geographical location, not to a specific congregation within that place. The letter was to all Christians in that place.

Our understanding of 'church' needs to move away from separate denominations or streams – a 'my church verses your church' mentality – towards a unified understanding. Where we are all Christians with different meetings in different buildings, yet together we are the Church in whatever geographical location we are in.

Unity was God's idea.

Let us do everything we can to build up the unity of the Church wherever we are.

Jesus, thank you for coming to the earth. Thank you for showing me the way back to God and for making it possible for me to get there through your death that paid the price for my sin. Thank you that unity was God's idea. Help me to promote and strengthen the unity that exists between the people in my church. Help me to get a wider view of your global church. I ask you to continue to build the unity between different churches, that we may truly behave as your unified body on the earth.
Amen.

DAY 6 – TOGETHER AS ONE

If then there is any encouragement in Christ, any consolation from love, any sharing in the Spirit, any compassion and sympathy, make my joy complete: be of the same mind, having the same love, being in full accord and of one mind. (Philippians 2:1-2)

I am no sportsman, although I do enjoy watching a good game of rugby from time to time. I remember watching the 1995 World Cup Rugby final. The competition was being hosted by South Africa and living in Zimbabwe, which did not really have a strong rugby team, we all supported the neighbouring country of South Africa. The final was a big deal at my senior school. We had rigged up a projector to the TV signal so we could watch the game on the big screen in the school hall.

It was an intense match as both teams were going all-out to beat their opponents. It could have gone either way right up until the dying minutes of the game when South Africa scored some points and defeated New Zealand against the odds. Not only did the South African team play as a unit, embodying true unity and single mindedness of purpose, their victory helped to bring unity across the nation that was only just emerging from a past of racism and division.

In today's Bible passage. Paul encourages the believers in Philippi to stand united as this is a reflection of the unity we experience between us and Christ. If we are united with Jesus, we are also united with fellow Christians. Therefore, we need to work towards being one in spirit and mind.

We should work together with our brothers and sisters in Christ – those within the same church, those from different churches, those from different countries. We are the family of God, called to work together for the gospel of Jesus.

Unity is much deeper than smiling at one another across the room or agreeing to advertise the church down the road's cake sale. We are called to live together in such a way that creates a symphony – a melodious melody made up of many different parts and instruments, all playing the same tune together in a synchronised way that achieves a beautiful result. This requires actually working together, putting aside differences so that the ultimate purpose of making Jesus known in our communities is realised.

This is not an easy task. It can only be achieved as we all embrace the example of humility, of putting others before ourselves, that Jesus showed us. And this is impossible if we try to do it without the help and empowerment of the one sent to help us, The Holy Spirit.

Just as the rugby team had to work together towards a common goal, we should work towards sharing the good news and love of Jesus. The rugby team were willing to suffer pain and hardship in their endeavour and refused to be afraid of the opposing team. We too should be willing to stand against the enemies of God, even if this means we will suffer because our prize is far greater than the World Cup trophy – it is Jesus himself.

Let us pause and consider our own situations and circumstances. What can we do to deepen the unity between ourselves and other Christians within our churches or wider communities? Are we willing to suffer to achieve this unity for the sake of Christ? Are we willing to allow the Holy Spirit to work in us and through us as we align our steps with His?

Jesus, I ask that you help me to promote unity amongst those in my church and in the wider Christian community around me. Help me to stand up for truth together with my brothers and sisters in Christ. Help me to refuse to be afraid of those who stand against us, knowing that You are in control. Jesus, help me to be willing to do what is necessary to further your kingdom, even if this means I may suffer.
Amen.

DAY 7 – PARTNERSHIP

When I remember you in my prayers, I always thank my God because I hear of your love for all the saints and your faith towards the Lord Jesus. I pray that the sharing of your faith may become effective when you perceive all the good that we may do for Christ. I have indeed received much joy and encouragement from your love, because the hearts of the saints have been refreshed through you, my brother. (Philemon 4-7)

Today, I want to focus in on the word 'we'. This is written in a letter sent a great distance. So, the togetherness expressed here is not physical. Instead, it recognises a bond, a partnership between writer and reader as they work together towards achieving the same goal – a partnership.

The word 'partner', like so many other words in the English language, has a variety of meanings and can be used in different ways.

The first is in terms of business where two or more people formally and legally agree to form a partnership. This means that they are in business together. They work together, take on risk together and ultimately share the profits of the business together.

The second relates to when a couple of people informally decide to work together or 'team up'. You can have a dance partner, for example.

The third articulates a more intimate relationship between two people. The term 'partner' can be applied to both married couples as well as unmarried.

In today's Bible passage, Paul is praying for an effective partnership between himself and Philemon's church. Notice how this partnership is made possible because of their shared faith in Jesus and that the result of their partnership is for the sake of Jesus – it is to bring glory to Jesus and to further His Kingdom.

We can also see that this partnership is ultimately beneficial for Philemon as he grows in spiritual maturity, he will come to know all the good things he has because of Jesus. In turn, Paul has benefitted through this relationship as he is extremely happy and encouraged by Philemon's love for him and for the wider church.

Partnership in its very essence is formed out of close relationship. If we are wanting to partner with someone or one church is wanting to partner with another church, it all begins with forming a strong relationship. It is so much more than just pooling our resources.

Once a relationship of mutual trust is established, then it becomes more possible to move together in a partnership. A relationship where cost, risk and effort are taken on by both parties and where reward is shared.

Taking the idea of partnership one step further, if we are wanting to partner with fellow Christians and churches to further the Kingdom of God and to share the good news of the gospel with others, we need to ensure that another all-important partnership is healthy and strong – our relationship with Jesus.

The Church is the Bride of Christ. We are supposed to be in an intimate partnership with Him.

Just as Paul acknowledges that his partnership with Philemon is based upon their shared love of Jesus, it is this relationship that is central for us as well. As we build our relationship with Jesus, allowing Him to lead us and guide us, we will be amazed that as we work together in partnership with others who are also obediently following Jesus with all their hearts, we all end up moving in the same direction together. It is our love of Jesus that makes unity in the Church possible.

If there is a problem with the unity between the people in our churches, let us encourage one another to first and foremost get our relationships with Jesus sorted out. And may this begin with us.

Jesus, thank you for giving me partners to help me live a life that is pleasing to You. Thank you that I don't need to do it alone. Help me to be a good partner, one that refreshes the hearts of the Lord's people like Philemon. Help me also to love you more. If there is a problem with our relationship, please let me know what it is and help me to change. Amen.

DAY 8 – GET ALONG

I urge Euodia and I urge Syntyche to be of the same mind in the Lord. Yes, and I ask you also, my loyal companion, help these women, for they have struggled beside me in the work of the gospel, together with Clement and the rest of my co-workers, whose names are in the book of life. (Philippians 4:2-3)

Have you ever found it hard to get along with someone in church? I know I have.

Sometimes personalities clash, or careless words are said. And sadly, on occasion, people who were once friends can fall out in a big way. Working and laughing together one day then not speaking and walking on the opposite sides of the street to each other the next.

It is best to sort problems out sooner rather than later. The longer something like this is left without being confronted and dealt with, it festers and causes bitterness to grow.

As with the case mentioned in today's passage, it is often difficult to deduce who caused offence first. But it is clear that offence has been taken on both sides – this is a problem as we are called to forgive and to bear with each other in love. Both Euodia and Syntyche are at fault in this regard.

Paul asks an unnamed person to intervene and to help restore the relationship between these two Christian women. Notice that their salvation is not lost due to their falling out, but they need help from a fellow believer to restore their relationship.

I have noticed too that within our current culture, it is extremely easy for anyone to take offence at the slightest thing and to then pursue this aggressively with a righteous indignation that leaves no room for disagreement or indeed for forgiveness.

We need to be careful that we are not shaped by the prevailing culture around us – we are meant to be shaped by Jesus.

We also need to create an atmosphere where we are free to disagree agreeably. Disagreement is going to happen. This is unavoidable. So, what do we do when it does happen? How will we react? If there is disagreement, how can we disagree with each other in an agreeable way?

If we seek to encourage others to see things in a different way, we need to start with ourselves.

Whether I am trying to show love to someone, to disagree agreeably, choosing not to take offence or I am doing my best to bear with someone, I can't control how they will behave towards me. They may not be in the same place as me spiritually (or have not read the same devotional as me). Where they are in their relationship with Jesus and how they react to situations is up to them. My relationship with Jesus and my behaviour is up to me. I cannot use how someone else reacts towards me as an excuse for my own bad behaviour. It starts with me.

It is up to us to model the way Jesus has asked us to live regardless of whether the other person we are finding difficult does so or not.

It is also wise to consider the possibility that we may also be in the wrong. That the person we find difficult may also find us extremely difficult too.

One of the best ways I have found to work towards restoring

broken relationships, yes even broken relationships between fellow Christians, is to pray for them. Prayer has an amazing power to reposition and humble us as well as giving the situation and the hearts of both the other person and ourselves over to God. It also gives the Holy Spirit permission to work on healing and changing us.

Are you finding someone difficult?

What can you pray for them today?

Jesus, help me to control my behaviour when I encounter people whom I find difficult. Help me to choose to love. Help me to forgive. Help me not to take offence. Help me to bear with my fellow Christian brother or sister with your help. I ask that you restore my relationships today so that we can truly be a unified church.

Amen.

DAY 9 – MAKE EVERY EFFORT

I therefore, the prisoner in the Lord, beg you to lead a life worthy of the calling to which you have been called, with all humility and gentleness, with patience, bearing with one another in love, making every effort to maintain the unity of the Spirit in the bond of peace. (Ephesians 4:1-3)

Over the years I have attempted a couple of dieting plans. My love of dessert is too great for the amount of energy I choose not to expend, and as a result, my waistband expands.

One thing I can say for the various dieting regimes out there is that for them to work, one needs to be dedicated. They take a lot of effort. Not only is it an overhaul of one's eating habits and portion sizes, they also involve some kind of additional exercise component in one form or another.

They can also be costly financially as paying a weekly or monthly subscription fee adds up. I suppose this financial commitment can be a powerful motivator and increase one's commitment to achieving the desired goal.

In today's Bible passage, Paul encourages the Ephesian Christians, and indeed all believers, to live lives worthy of the calling they have received. He doesn't just leave this as an unexplained mystery, as he goes on to explain how to live in this way.

He encourages them, as well as us, to live lives of love as it is from living lovingly that the unity between them will grow and flourish.

And how are we to live loving lives? By being humble, gentle, patient and by bearing with one another.

The biggest secret ingredient of unity is humility[1]. Taking the view of preferring others above the interests of oneself. Or indeed, reaching loving compromise based upon our mutual love for Jesus over and above organisational structures or operational systems. Without humility, unity will be very hard to achieve and maintain.

By treating each other with patience and gentleness, we can create an atmosphere where unity can flourish.

Paul warns us that pursuing unity will take a lot of effort. Just as my attempts at dieting showed me how much dedication and hard work play their part in helping one to achieve successful results, so to with unity amongst believers in Jesus.

It is the Holy Spirit who creates the unity, but we are responsible for maintaining it[2], and this is not easy. But neither is it impossible.

Paul continues this theme in his letter to the Colossians where again he says that the unity amongst those who believe in Jesus will be reflected in the peace that exists between them (Colossians 3:14-15). Peace is the chord that binds and holds us together.

Let us pause and consider what this looks like in our contexts today.

Are we putting in the required effort and energy into maintaining the unity that exists within our churches, and within the wider church we are part of?

Are we basing our unity on our shared love of Jesus or are the ways we do things creating barriers?

Are we being humble or is pride getting in the way?

Or is our unity a bit like a yo-yo diet that works for a short time, but then after a while momentum and the will to succeed is lost and we end up right back where we started?

Is this what Paul was warning us against?

Let us acknowledge that maintaining unity is a huge task and is impossible without the empowering of the Holy Spirit. However, we need to be willing and determined to see it through so that we too can live lives worthy of the calling we have received.

Jesus, unity is hard work. Give me the endurance and the patience to continue to pursue unity with others in the church. Help me to have a humble spirit, to be gentle and to bear with others better. Help me to live a life of love in thought, word and deed and may the bond of peace created by our unity continue to grow stronger.
Amen.

DAY 10 – UNIFIED AROUND CHRIST

We must no longer be children, tossed to and fro and blown about by every wind of doctrine, by people's trickery, by their craftiness in deceitful scheming. But speaking the truth in love, we must grow up in every way into him who is the head, into Christ. (Ephesians 4:14-15)

I have three children.

The eldest is now seven. She is growing into a kind and caring person full of empathy and love for others. She is currently battling to learn her multiplication tables and finds piano practise difficult from time to time, especially if she is just starting to learn how to play a new piece of music.

Her sister is just a couple of years younger. She has just started primary school and is learning about the letters of the alphabet and the sounds they make. She eagerly traces the letters as she practises forming them when we sit together in the evenings. She is also enjoying counting and is just beginning to learn the basics of mathematics.

Their younger brother has just turned two. He is learning how to talk and seems to add a new word to his vocabulary every day, although his most used word is still 'no'. He loves playing with toy cars and watching the tractors in the fields just outside the window. He likes his food too, although he has not yet managed to master the use of a spoon.

It is clear from the passage that as Christians, we are supposed to be growing. Not growing in terms of how a tree grows by increasing its size, but more accurately, we should be growing up. We begin as infants and then as we learn and as our relationship with Jesus develops, we begin to change and mature.

As my children grow and go through the various stages of life, they are a joy to watch. Being involved in their growth and learning is an enormous privilege.

As Christians we should be maturing and becoming more like Jesus. Spiritual growth takes time but unlike natural maturation, it is not inevitable. It requires work and dedication. We need to make decisions every day to do things Jesus' way and not our own.

We have already encountered the metaphor where the church is compared to a human body – living, breathing and consisting of many parts (see Day 3). But here we are told that it is in fact Jesus who is the head of this body. Jesus is the head of the Church. It is because of Jesus that our unity exists in the first place as everything comes from Him and is joined and held together because of Him.

The head contains the brain, the control centre of the body. Your leg will only move because the brain has sent a signal telling it to do so. Likewise, if your brain does not push a nerve impulse to your mouth to make it eat, you won't eat.

In the same way, as individual body parts and the Church as the entire body of Christ, we should be responding to the head – to Jesus.

We should be tuned in to what Jesus is asking us to do, and then we should be doing it.

Not only this, but as we come to recognise Jesus at work within other believers and other churches, we can much more easily follow what He is asking us to do. With Jesus taking the lead, we can work together in fulfilling our calling and mission because of the unity that already exists between us because of the love of Christ.

Jesus, help me to respond to you. Help me to follow where you lead me. To love my brothers and sisters around me even if they are vastly different from me, knowing that we have you in common. Thank you that unity is your idea and that you make it possible.
Amen.

FURTHER READING &
QUESTIONS 2

EPHESIANS 1-3

Wider Reading – Unity

Jesus Prays for Unity - John 17:20-23

How to Live in Unity - Colossians 3:11-17

All Children of God - Galatians 3:26-29

Unity is Good and Pleasant - Psalm 133

Discussion Questions – Unity

What makes it easy or difficult to view the collection of local churches in your area as being 'The Church' rather than a group of different churches?

What would need to change or be encouraged to help widen people's view of the Church and their place within it?

Can you identify any positives or bonds of unity that already exist between local churches in your area?

Can you identify any barriers to unity? What would need to be done to help overcome these?

Read Colossians 3:11-17. Is this helpful instruction on how to live in unity with one another?

Is there anything else that may be helpful that you would like to add to this list?

Is there anyone whom you are finding difficult at the moment? What can you pray about for this person and for yourself to help restore relationship and strengthen unity between you?

PART III

SPIRITUAL WARFARE

DAY 11 – JESUS VICTORIOUS

And when you were dead in trespasses and the uncircumcision of your flesh, God made you alive together with him, when he forgave us all our trespasses, erasing the record that stood against us with its legal demands. He set this aside, nailing it to the cross. He disarmed the rulers and authorities and made a public example of them, triumphing over them in it. (Colossians 2:13-15)

I used to be a primary school teacher. I was an employee, so I had to do what my boss asked me to do. Some of it was tedious, some of it was difficult, some of it was horrible. There were some good and pleasant things too. If something went wrong, I would have to explain myself. I might even be disciplined if I did something really terrible.

My boss had power over me as an employee. I had signed a contract agreeing to work for that school and had legally agreed to do what they asked of me. However, when I resigned and the day came when I was no longer employed by that school, my boss had no power over me anymore. I no longer had to do what they asked me to do. I did not have to turn up to work on time – in fact it would be very strange if I turned up for work at all after having left the job.

As we begin this chapter on spiritual warfare, I think it important to establish who holds the ultimate power and who does not.

Lent is a time of reflection and sometimes even for fasting. But it is also a time for remembering the love of God shown to us through the death and resurrection of Jesus, and the ultimate defeat of death, sin and Satan. I have saved the final chapter for a more detailed look at this, but actually the entire book rests on this foundational cornerstone.

When thinking about spiritual warfare, we first need to remember that the big battle has already been won.

Jesus died.

Jesus rose again.

It is finished!

He has disarmed the spiritual powers and authorities. We are no longer bound by our old contract of living sinfully that we inherited by virtue of being a human born into a broken and sinful world. We have already been set free from sin by the finished work of Christ on the cross.

When we chose to give our lives to Jesus, we were made new in Him. The old self under the old contract was destroyed and our new re-born selves came into being. Our spirit was made alive inside us, and we were empowered by the Holy Spirit – God's power at work living and working in us and though us.

Jesus has already won the ultimate victory. Satan is defeated. Yes, he is waiting for the day of judgement when we will all be judged, and he wants to take as many of us down with him as he can. There are still battles going on, but we are fighting a defeated foe.

World War I officially ended on 11th November 1918 at 11am but different countries agreed to peace at different times. Indeed, in certain places, fighting continued for a while after the armistice had been agreed.[1]

Similarly, Satan and his demons are still fighting battles and we are still engaged in a spiritual war even though he is already defeated.

We should approach spiritual warfare from a position of the victory we have in Jesus. We have the upper hand. We are in a position of strength and we have the power and authority of the risen Christ working in us and through us and no force of hell can stand against it.

Jesus, thank You for your victory on the cross, that you have won the war for us all. Please help me to remember my position that I have as your child – a position of strength and authority.
Amen

DAY 12 – STAND FIRM

Only, live your life in a manner worthy of the gospel of Christ, so that, whether I come and see you or am absent and hear about you, I will know that you are standing firm in one spirit, striving side by side with one mind for the faith of the gospel, and are in no way intimidated by your opponents. For them this is evidence of their destruction, but of your salvation. And this is God's doing. (Philippians 1:27-28)

'Gaining Ground' is the name given to a rugby training drill that I used to play in primary school. I am notoriously bad at sports, so I may not be recalling it correctly. But I recall this game being played in two teams. You started off in the middle of the rugby pitch and one side kicked the ball as high and as far as they could into the territory, or the half of the field of their opponents. The opposing team had to catch the ball or stop it from rolling as soon as they could. They then returned the kick from wherever they were able to stop the ball. This is also where the new territory line for each team was drawn.

If you were bad at catching or stopping the ball, the other team's territory kept increasing as they moved further and further into their opponent's half of the field. The game ended when one team managed to kick the ball over their opponent's try line at the back of the pitch. All the opponent's ground had been gained by the other team.

When looking at the subject of spiritual warfare, there is a lot of mention of 'standing firm'.

Just as Paul emphasised the fact that Jesus has already won the ultimate victory over Satan in his letter to the church in Colossae that we looked at yesterday, he now mentions it to the church in Philippi.

He instructs them to stand firm and to do so by standing together, as one. Again, the importance of unity is stressed and indeed shown as a vital component to effective spiritual warfare.

They are to stand in the position of power and strength that the victory of Christ gives them and that they can access because as followers of Jesus they are now 'in Christ' – just as we who believe today are.

It is clear from Paul's letter here that opposition and suffering is inevitable. But when it comes, we need to pull together and not be afraid of those who oppose us.

In the middle of it all, we are also called to live lives that are beyond reproach. Lives that are worthy of the gospel of Jesus. What an impossible task. But then again, isn't this the point? It is impossible for us to live so perfectly in and through our own strength. We can only attempt to do so through the power of Jesus. We are now 'in Christ' and the Holy Spirit is living and working within us, transforming us, and helping us to become more and more like Christ each day.

We need to understand that this transformation to Christlikeness is a gradual process. It is also a continual process that will last until the day we die, as true Christlikeness is impossible this side of eternity. And yes, we may even fail and fall. But we need to keep coming back to Jesus, dust ourselves off and choose to stand once again in the power of His Spirit.

And as we do this, it acts as a sign to our opponents that Jesus is alive; Jesus is in charge; Jesus is at work in us and because of this, they are inevitably going to lose the fight.

So, when we stand firm, we are not standing on enemy ground. We are standing on solid ground that has already been won by Jesus on our behalf.

When the enemy is throwing everything at us, or kicking rugby balls into our territory, we can rest assured that Jesus is in control. We can stand and not give an inch of ground away to the enemy. We have a star player on our team who is better at catching and kicking than anyone on the face of the earth. Our win is guaranteed, and it is our opponents who should be worried about losing their ground because the Kingdom of God is forcefully advancing with Jesus as our captain and star player.

So, as we start to think about spiritual warfare let us remember who we are in Christ and what has already been accomplished for us by Jesus on the cross.

There may be areas in our lives where we wish we could stand firm. Let's ask Jesus to help us to do just that today.

Jesus, you are the star player on my team. I cannot stand firm without you. You know the areas in my life where I find it hard to live the life you have called me to live, a life worthy of the gospel. Help me to live that way through your Holy Spirit who is alive and at work within me today.
Amen.

DAY 13 – WHERE THE BATTLE RAGES

For our struggle is not against enemies of blood and flesh, but against the rulers, against the authorities, against the cosmic powers of this present darkness, against the spiritual forces of evil in the heavenly places. Therefore take up the whole armour of God, so that you may be able to withstand on that evil day, and having done everything, to stand firm. (Ephesians 6:12-13)

My grandfather fought in World War II. He was a member of the Royal Air Force and was a navigator aboard a Lancaster bomber aircraft. Our family has always found this job role somewhat surprising because his sense of direction was terrible. Needless to say, he survived the war and went on to marry my grandmother.

It is important that soldiers know where the battle they are supposed to be fighting is located. If not, there could be dire consequences. Incorrect targets could be attacked, and innocent people could be killed.

It is equally important for us as Christians to know where the battle is. From the moment we believed in Jesus and chose to give our lives over to His service, we were conscripted into his holy army.

We should be under no illusion – we are engaged in an epic war between good and evil. The fight is on.

But we need to know where the primary battle is raging in order for us to be effective soldiers in the fight. It is happening in the spiritual dimension, and this impacts us here in the physical realm. The two are interlinked.

Firstly, we need to understand that the spiritual dimension is not somewhere far away floating on a cloud but is up close. It is all around us. Sometimes we catch a glimpse of it, or we have a sense of its presence. In fact, the spiritual dimension is interwoven with the physical. This is how prayers made in the spiritual realm are answered in the physical. Things we do in the physical dimension can impact the spiritual dimension and the same can also be true in reverse.

Secondly, as Paul tells us, we need to know that it is in the spiritual dimension where the battle is taking place. Things may be happening in the physical realm that try to demand our attention. Yet another illness befalls the family; the bills are mounting up and will be a struggle to pay and then the washing machine breaks down; a world leader does some unspeakable act; we fall out with a friend, or someone writes unkind comments about us on the internet – all these things can be difficult and painful, but we need to remember where the real fight is taking place.

Thirdly, we need to know what the battle is. Our battle is to see what God wants to happen, happen. To do God's will. To spread His Kingdom. To pierce the darkness of brokenness and sin around us with the light of his truth and love.

Every soldier needs armour and weapons in order for them to carry out their role effectively. The same is true for us. We are engaged in a spiritual war, so we have been supplied with spiritual weapons and armour. It's no good just being given the equipment, we need to pick it up. We need to put it on, and we need to use it.

Without shielding ourselves with the spiritual armour and wielding the spiritual sword God has supplied for us, we will be defenceless against Satan and his minions. We will find ourselves chasing conspiracy theories and trying to land the blame for all sorts of things all over the place. We will be attacking incorrect targets and innocent people will be caught in the crossfire of our misdirected assumptions.

It may be as you read these words, the Holy Spirit has started to show you areas in your life where you have been fighting against the physical manifestation of a spiritual reality. You have been focusing your attack on the wrong place. I have done this many times and have needed the Holy Spirit to redirect me back to where the battle was truly raging – in the spirit.

Jesus, thank you that you are on my side. Thank you that you haven't left me helpless or defenceless in this spiritual fight. Please open my eyes to reality of the spiritual battle and help me to know how I can fight effectively as your follower. Help me not to be distracted by things in the physical dimension that may try to take my focus away from where the battle truly is.
Help me Jesus.
Amen.

DAY 14 – TRUTH & RIGHTEOUSNESS

Stand therefore, and fasten the belt of truth around your waist, and put on the breastplate of righteousness. (Ephesians 6:14)

As Paul was in prison while writing this letter, he had Roman soldiers guarding him. He was easily able to relate spiritual things to the physical metaphor their armour provided as it was right in front of him.

The first piece mentioned is the belt of truth[1]. I don't think this is an accident. The belt gathers and holds everything together in the right place and helps it work effectively. In the same way, we need to know what the truth is for the other pieces of the armour to be effective.

Would you buy a fake motorcycle helmet or a fake seatbelt? It may be cheaper, but it would be completely useless and potentially lethal. In the same way, we need to ensure that we are not wearing fake armour – believing things that are not true.

In today's culture of 'relative truth' - where you can believe whatever you like, just as long as you don't expect me to believe it too - absolute truth is rejected. Yet absolute truth is what we need.

How do we discern what real truth is? We need to know the word of truth (the truths we receive through the Bible) and the person of truth (Jesus). Together they can help us to really know what truth is and this means we need to spend time with them both on a regular basis. The more we get to see, touch and know the genuine article, the more easily we will be able to spot a fake when it comes along.

The next piece of armour is the breastplate of righteousness[2] - today's equivalent would be a bullet-proof vest as it too protects the body's vital organs in a similar way.

There are two aspects to righteousness that would be helpful for us to understand.

The first is the righteousness we can only find in and through Jesus, that is, us being in 'right standing' with God. A righteousness that can only come through us having faith in Jesus and what he has done for us on the cross and not based on anything we have done at all, as Paul explains in Philippians 3:7-10.

Knowing that we are forgiven of our sin and can approach God based on Jesus having paid our debt through his death on the cross takes the power away from Satan, the accuser, when he comes to taunt us with failure, anxiety, and guilt. We do not owe him anything anymore. We are made new in Jesus and stand upon His righteousness alone.

The second is the righteousness worked within us by the work of the Holy Spirit. The integrity and morality He helps us attain. Now, instead of succumbing to temptation which used to be our default response before choosing to follow Jesus, we can now choose to respond differently.

At salvation a giant shift happens in the spirit. We are re-born, and our spirit is made alive within us. This leads to real and practical change in the way in which we live our lives. We won't completely change overnight, it is a process, but one change will lead to another as we start to be transformed and gradually become more and more like Jesus. This happens as we daily choose Jesus' ways instead of our own.

Let us take some time today and connect with Jesus, the person of truth, as well as read and think about the Bible, the word of truth, so that we can more easily identify any lies or deceptions when they appear.

Change is a key indicator of salvation. Let's spend some time reflecting upon what our lives used to be like before we chose to follow Jesus and what they are like now. Let us give thanks for the change and the progress we have seen as we become more and more like Jesus.

Jesus, you are the person of truth. You know what is true and what is a lie. Help me to trust you, to hear your voice and to respond to you. Help me to understand the truth as shown to us in the Bible. Thank you that you freely give your righteousness to me. That because of you and your sacrifice, I can stand in the presence of God and have a relationship with him. Holy Spirit, continue working in my life, changing me to be more and more like Jesus. Thank you for how you have already changed me and help me to work together with you to change me even more.
Amen.

DAY 15 – FAITH & THE GOSPEL

As shoes for your feet put on whatever will make you ready to proclaim the gospel of peace. With all of these, take the shield of faith, with which you will be able to quench all the flaming arrows of the evil one. (Ephesians 6:15-16)

I do not envy the chiropodist's job – having to deal with smelly, sweaty feet. Some with callouses, bits of dead skin and whatever-it-is that gets caught in between your toes!

No matter what our feet are like, they too need protecting.

Being a father of three young children, I live in constant dread of accidentally stepping on any small, sharp toys that are often left strewn on the living room carpet. Have you ever stepped on a small plastic building brick without shoes on before? It's not an experience you want to have, believe me.

If our feet are incapacitated by an attack, or by a small plastic building brick, we writhe about in pain and any progress of standing against an attack or indeed of moving forward on the offensive is abruptly halted. This is why shoes were invented. They protect our feet, helping us to stay standing. They also provide grip, helping us to advance and move forward[1].

Our spiritual shoes are fitted with readiness. We are to be prepared for the battle. Spiritual warfare should not come as any surprise. We need to be ready.

And this readiness comes from the gospel of peace. We need to be sure of the gospel and believe it. Not only that, but we also need to be living in its power every day. Believing in Jesus, the Son of God who died to forgive our sin and who rose again to everlasting life. Repenting of our sin as a result - a changing of our minds and therefore our behaviour. This means we should know that we are free from the slavery of sin. We can resist temptation and are eager and ready to tell others how they can become free too.

This results in us being at peace with God, as through the gospel we are no longer His enemies. It also brings peace within ourselves and with one another.

We are also told to pick up our shield of faith.

Faith can be used to protect us from any number of the enemy's spiritual attacks (flaming arrows) such as doubt, fear, temptation, false teaching etc. The Roman shield was almost as tall as a human body, so the shield would protect most of the vital organs, including the heart.

Unlike other parts of the armour already mentioned that are already attached to the body, we need to actively pick up our shield of faith. We need to choose to believe God's promises and His ways in every situation.

Roman shields could be also used as a weapon, with the metallic convex or conical boss attached to the front of it being used to hit against opponents. They could also be joined together to form an impregnable barrier, those at the front making a moveable wall and those behind creating a roof that the soldiers stood underneath – like a tortoise shell.

Working together, embracing unity with our brothers and sisters in Christ. Raising up our shields of faith, we too can create a highly effective and mobile unit that not only defends but also enables forward movement.

Faith and the gospel seem to go together like a hand and a glove. You need to have faith to believe and the strength of our belief in turn reinforces our faith.

Let us be sure we know what the gospel is.

Let us be sure to live out what we believe in thought and word and deed.

Let us have faith in Jesus and in the promises and resources of God.

Let us put on our shoes and pick up our shields so that we are ready when the attack comes.

Jesus, thank you for the faith you have given me. I choose to believe. I believe you are God's only son, that you died and rose again. I believe I have been set free because you have already paid the price for my sin. Help me to believe and have faith even when the attack comes. May I be ready. Help me to stand my ground.
Amen

DAY 16 – SALVATION & THE WORD OF GOD

Take the helmet of salvation, and the sword of the Spirit, which is the word of God. (Ephesians 6:17)

A lot of the spiritual battles we face take place in the mind. Our thoughts can quite literally be a minefield. We are very often attacked through our thoughts as they can lead to behaviour if acted upon. Consistent behaviours can become habits. And habits form character.

Our brains are the control-centre of our entire bodies. Our minds need protecting from the onslaught of the enemy. Therefore, we have been supplied with a helmet - the helmet of salvation[1]. When we are in the heat of the battle, we need to know that we are saved. Indeed, all other parts of the armour rely upon our understanding of our salvation and our new position in Christ.

We need to rely completely upon Jesus and the salvation He freely gives to us. We cannot save ourselves. Indeed, we need to constantly evaluate our thinking. If our thoughts line up with what God says about things, we can allow them in. If they contradict what God says is right and true, we need to allow those thoughts to bounce off our helmets – don't give them any time, or any further headspace (2 Corinthians 10:5).

Now that we believe in Jesus and have given our lives to Him, we need to allow our thinking to be changed by Him (Romans 12:2). We should be desiring to think His thoughts and not our own because we don't naturally have the same thoughts as God, nor do we see things so easily from His perspective (Isaiah 55:8).

So, we have been given spiritual armour, which is mostly defensive. A protection from attack. However, we have also been given a spiritual weapon – the sword of the spirit, which as Paul explains here is the word of God.

When I first read this, my immediate thought was 'Ah yes, the Bible. The Bible is my weapon.' However, a closer look at the Greek language that this letter was originally written in reveals that there are two words that both translate into English as 'word'.

There is the 'logos' word and the 'rhema' word[2].

The 'logos' word refers to the established and written word of God. It has also been used in reference to Jesus himself, being the Word of God established before the creation of the world. Whereas the 'rhema' word speaks of what is happening now. It describes what God is doing or saying to a specific person in a certain situation. It is a word that is released in the power and Spirit of God and is alive and active now, in the moment.

In this passage 'rhema' is used when describing the sword of the spirit.

It is worth noting that both the rhema and logos word are interlinked and rely upon each other. One will not contradict the other, but support and strengthen what is being said in both ways.

So, we do need to know what the Bible says. We do need to read it. However, the weapon in our hands is the living power of God, the Holy Spirit alive and active working within us and through us to fight effectively. We are engaged in a supernatural battle, so we need supernatural weapons to fight with. And who better to be on our side, leading and guiding us and fighting in us and through us, but the very living power, person and presence of God himself – the Holy Spirit.

Again, relationship is vital. We need to be talking with God and listening and responding to God. Our relationship needs to be fresh and vibrant in order for us to be moving in the rhema word of God at all times – equipped and ready to fight. It is a lot less about following written down rules and regulations and a lot more about allowing God to be in charge and allowing Him to exercise His power through us.

It takes effort to use a sword. It also takes practise.

Are we practicing the presence of God regularly by spending time with Him, hearing his rhema word and acting upon it?

Let's spend some time in His presence today.

Jesus, help me to take captive every though and make it obedient to you. May your salvation be the basis upon which I build my entire life. Help me to walk closer to you each day. Help our relationship to be vital and fresh so that through the power of your Holy Spirit, I can be effective in the fight.
Amen

FURTHER READING & QUESTIONS 3

EPHESIANS 4-6

Wider Reading – Spiritual Warfare

Armour in Old Testament - Isaiah 59: 15b-17

God is our Fortress - Psalm 91

Righteousness from God - Philippians 3:7-10

Jesus is the Truth - John 14:6

Truth of Scripture - 2 Timothy 3:16-17

Spiritual Weapons - 2 Corinthians 10:4-6

Fruit of the Spirit - Galatians 5:22

Discussion Questions – Spiritual Warfare

How important is it for us to know that Jesus has already won the ultimate victory?

What would change if we did not know this?

How can we act differently because of this truth?

If we are fighting a spiritual battle, does this mean we don't respond or do anything when we are physically attacked, or taken to court, or someone writes nasty things about us on the internet?

Should we fight back, and if so, how should we do this?

Is there such a thing as absolute truth and if so, how do we know what it is?

If so, how can we live in a world where this notion is often rejected?

Read Galatians 5:22. To what extent can we view the fruit of the Spirit as being spiritual weapons?

PART IV

PRAYER

DAY 17 – PRAY. PRAY. PRAY.

Pray in the Spirit at all times in every prayer and supplication. To that end keep alert and always persevere in supplication for all the saints. Pray also for me, so that when I speak, a message may be given to me to make known with boldness the mystery of the gospel, for which I am an ambassador in chains. Pray that I may declare it boldly, as I must speak. (Ephesians 6:18-20)

There is a beach on the North Norfolk Coast of England about an hour's drive away from where I live. When I go there on the occasional beach trip with the family in the summer months there are often scores of kite surfers on the water. They are pulled along and often lifted right out of the water by their kite that is attached to their waists by strong cables. It is quite fun to watch, although I must admit, I prefer to leave the kite surfing to the enthusiasts.

Prayer can be a bit like kite surfing.

The kite surfer needs to keep the wind full in the sail so they can be propelled along the water. In the same way, we need to keep our lives full of the Holy Spirit so we can be led and propelled forwards in our relationship with Jesus. If the wind dies, the sail crumples and falls and the kite surfer ends up in the water. The same can happen to us if we neglect prayer.

Paul encourages the Ephesian church to 'pray in the Spirit at all times in every prayer and supplication.'

We need to pray at all times. Prayer, in conjunction with the Holy Spirit, is the connection that keeps our relationship with Jesus alive. It also keeps us relying upon Him and His power to accomplish the things He has called us to do and to stand firm when an attack comes.

Being attached to our kite means that we are able to face and ride the waves whenever trouble comes. We need to keep firmly attached to Jesus so that we can follow Him wherever He may lead and so that our armour will be effective in times of attack.

Simply put, prayer is communication. It is how we talk to Jesus and how Jesus communicates with us. It is not supposed to be anything complicated or fancy. Prayers do not have to be written down in advance, although some may find this useful. And prayer certainly does not need to be loaded with religious language – just speak plainly to Jesus in your own voice with your own words.

There are many types of prayer that include: adoration, petition, intercession, contemplation, confession, silence, listening, lamenting and much more besides. (To dig deeper into types of prayer I recommend reading 'How To Pray' by Pete Greig - 2019, Hodder & Stoughton, and '7 Ways to Pray' by Amy Boucher Pye - 2021, SPCK).

Jesus hears us when we pray. Do we give space and time for us to hear from Him?

In Christian circles you can often hear the phrase 'Jesus said to me...', or 'God told me...' Although an audible voice is sometimes heard on the rare occasion, hearing a voice speaking is not necessarily the norm. Often when people say this, they mean that Jesus has communicated with them through the Holy Spirit in some way. It could be that a particular Bible verse particularly struck them as they read it and they somehow knew that it was speaking directly into their situation. Or they may have seen a picture in their mind and understood it to be an answer to something they had been praying about. Or they just had a sense of peace within them when praying about a particular issue – you get the idea.

I don't claim to know how prayer works I just know that it does! Although its workings are a mystery, prayer is a very practical thing that anyone can do.

Prayer should become a natural part of every aspect of our lives and encompass all that we do. This in turn will lead us to praying a whole variety of prayers as we go through our day.

As we continue through the week, we will see that Paul prays a lot. He talks about prayer a lot and encourages fellow Christians to do the same. But we also see here that even though he is a well respected church leader, he is not afraid or ashamed to ask for prayer for himself.

He knows that prayer is powerful, and that prayer works because it is communication with Jesus. It aligns our will with Jesus' and the power of God can work through it.

Let us take some time to pray today.

Jesus, thank you that I can pray to you. Thank you that you hear me when we do. Help me to make prayer something that I always do. Give me the words I need – Lord, teach me to pray.
Amen.

DAY 18 – PRAY WITH CONFIDENCE

Yes, and I will continue to rejoice, for I know that through your prayers and the help of the Spirit of Jesus Christ this will result in my deliverance. (Philippians 1:18-19)

An unexpected demand from a debt collection agency landed on my doormat one day. At first, I thought it was a scam, but after some research I learnt that it was genuine and that I was in trouble with the law. I discovered someone had fraudulently used my identity to register a car, and then did not pay the road tax.

Unbeknown to me the case had already gone to court, and I was now expected to pay thousands of pounds to the DVLA in penalties and fines.

I told my church family about the situation, and they were praying for a just outcome. I appealed the court's initial decision made in my absence and finally got my day in court before a Magistrate where it was decided that in light of the evidence I provided, I was not the owner of the car and the charges against me were dropped.

Paul was also in trouble with the authorities of his day. He was being held under house arrest, imprisoned because he had been preaching about Jesus. The church in Philippi had been praying for Paul and this, together with the Holy Spirit actively at work, caused Paul to rejoice as he knew that he would be saved from his imprisonment. He knew that because those believers were praying for him, he would have sufficient courage to face his situation and looked forward to his release, either through death or acquittal (verse 20).

It is easy to grow weary when we pray for people, especially when the results of our prayers are not immediate. We need to be praying for God's will to be done in the situation, and not what we think the best outcome should be. God is the one who ultimately knows what is best in any given situation, no matter how bleak or desperate. His view is not restricted by time, like ours is. He can see beyond the present situation and can see the big picture. We need to trust that He knows what He is doing.

We should persist faithfully as our prayers are effective and the Holy Spirit is at work. We can trust God that he can use any situation for the good of those who love Him according to His purposes.

We can pray with confidence because we have confidence in the one to whom we pray.

Jesus is in control. He has already won the ultimate victory and Satan can't do anything about it.

When we pray, we need to remember this.

We don't need to shout and scream at Satan. We don't need to try to work ourselves up into a spiritual frenzy to help our prayers be more effective.

We need to understand that Jesus, who is the King of all kings in spiritual places and on earth, has delegated His authority to us. We stand in the rock solid position of His authority and power as His ambassadors. We speak with that same authority, and it carries the same weight.

Wow.

Paul had confidence in the prayers of his fellow Christians. We need to have confidence in the authority that Jesus has given us.

So, when we pray today, let us do so with perseverance and certainty – knowing that God hears our prayers. Let's also be brave enough to leave the outcome of our prayer to the divine will of God.

Jesus, help me to understand the identity I have as a child of God. May I grow in courage and boldness as this understanding grows. Help me to stand in the solid position of the victory you have already won for me as I pray for... I give them to you and ask that Your will be done in their lives.

Amen.

DAY 19 – PRAY BIG PRAYERS

For this reason, since the day we heard it, we have not ceased praying for you and asking that you may be filled with the knowledge of God's will in all spiritual wisdom and understanding, so that you may lead lives worthy of the Lord, fully pleasing to him, as you bear fruit in every good work and as you grow in the knowledge of God. May you be made strong with all the strength that comes from his glorious power, and may you be prepared to endure everything with patience, while joyfully giving thanks to the Father, who has enabled you to share in the inheritance of the saints in the light. (Colossians 1:9-12)

Speaking to my seven year old daughter, it amazes me how optimistic she is. She has BIG dreams and aspirations.

She wants to skateboard at the Olympics, sing on the stage at music festivals and become a famous painter – and this I imagine she hopes to achieve before she has finished eating her cereal in the morning!

I hope that in a few years' time, her dreams will be just as big as they are today.

But isn't it sad how the realities of life can start to make our dreams smaller? We begin to understand the impossible nature of things, or we realise how much hard work the dream requires for success, so we give up trying.

This view of life can also sadly encroach on our understanding of God.

We see the impossibility of a situation or can't think of any way we could overcome a challenge or hardship; we start to think that God sees it like this too.

How wrong we can be sometimes.

One of the beauties of prayer is that it can lift our gaze off ourselves, off the problem or the circumstances and turn our eyes towards Jesus. It is here, when we are looking at Him, that we can start to get a glimpse of how He sees things. His perspective carries hope and possibility. It starts to reveal freedom and light into situations where we could only see the darkness.

In today's passage from Paul's letter to the church in Colossae, we see him praying big prayers for his fellow Christians and friends. He is not looking at the impossibility of the circumstances he is in, or indeed his fellow Christians are in. No. He is looking at the God who can make impossible things possible.

Paul prays that they be continually filled with all knowledge and wisdom that comes from the Holy Spirit because this will enable them to live lives that are pleasing to Jesus in *every way*. This includes being fruitful with good works, growing in the knowledge of God and their discipleship, being strengthened with *all power* that comes from God so that they will be able to endure, have patience and give thanks to God who has done everything needed so that they can share in a life that is in relationship with Him both now and for eternity.

This big prayer encompasses the entire Christian life. It asks God to be at work in the lives of those believers, growing and building them to become more like Christ, filling them with the Holy Spirit, equipping them with wisdom and discernment to live life well and even looks ahead to living life eternally with God.

It would be great to be able to pray like this too – to pray big, bold prayers that seem to ask for the impossible.

And we can.

We could begin by asking God to expand our minds and our faith so that we can start to see things from his perspective, where we start to see the possibilities that are hiding within impossible things. And then we can start to speak them out. To pray prayers filled with hope, with intention and with life. Prayers that are bursting with light and love. Prayers that change the atmosphere, break strongholds and release the kingdom of God into any situation.

Jesus, help me to pray big prayers. Help me to see things from your perspective. Change my heart and my mind. Help me to boldly proclaim your love and restoration to those who are broken and hurting. Help me to see what you see in people and help me to pray that your kingdom come in their lives. Give me the words when I have none.
Amen.

DAY 20 – PRAY FOR OTHERS

In our prayers for you we always thank God, the Father of our Lord Jesus Christ, for we have heard of your faith in Christ Jesus and of the love that you have for all the saints (Colossians 1:3-4)

I'm sure many of us who own a mobile phone have taken a 'selfie' before – a photograph of ourselves that we have taken by holding the camera at arm's length and clicking the button. Or you may have taken the next step and have acquired a 'selfie stick' to help you take photos that show more of the scenery behind you or can fit in more friends or family members. This requires further distance from your body than what your arm alone can provide, so the aid of a stick is enlisted to extend the length the camera can be held away from your body. A helpful button on the stick is then pushed to tell the phone to take the photo.

How times have changed.

When I was younger, I took an old 'wind-up' camera with me on a weeklong school mountain hiking trip when I was about fifteen years old. Showing the photographs to my mother some months later, she remarked how nice the scenery was, because that is all I had taken pictures of. There were a couple of shots of my fellow classmates, but most of them were of waterfalls, and spectacular mountain views. I don't think the idea of taking a 'selfie' was invented yet. Besides, you could not see where exactly you were pointing the camera if you were holding it at arm's length and pointing it at yourself, and the film and its developing were expensive, so you didn't waste shots like that.

Throughout the prison letters, we see many examples, such as the passage today, where Paul prays for others. He celebrates the faith of others and brings their needs before God. He continually asks God to help others to grow in their discipleship.

These prayers were written in letters that were sent to those Paul was praying for, so served as an encouragement to them too, that Paul was letting them know that he was praying on their behalf.

Knowing that someone is praying for you can be a powerful thing.

I am sure Paul also prayed for himself and indeed he asks for prayer a few times too. Prayer is such a vital part of his instruction on how to live well as a Christian that I am certain he also prayed for his own needs as well as simply had conversations with Jesus.

The thing to notice here is that it is his prayers for others that come front and centre. Praying for others was more important than praying from himself. He made a fuss about praying for others – he had the camera pointed away from himself and had his selfie stick firmly locked away.

This is not to belittle prayers for ourselves. In fact, praying for ourselves and communicating with God about our lives is a vital part of continuing to build relationship with Him. The ebb and flow of a conversation - times when we talk, and times when we listen. Praying for ourselves has its place, but so does praying for others.

Perhaps we need to shift our priorities when we pray. Do we pray for others before we pray for ourselves, or do our own needs and worries come tumbling out first? Are we praying 'selfie' prayers where our focus and attention is all on ourselves, or are we praying prayers where the needs of others come first and prayers for ourselves come second?

Let us pray for someone else today.

Jesus, help me to pray for others like Paul did. Help me to give thanks for my fellow Christians' spiritual growth and progress. Please remind me when I need to rearrange my priorities when I pray, so that my prayers for others come before prayers for myself. Help me to lock my prayer 'selfie stick' away so that my focus and attention can be in the right place.
Amen.

DAY 21 – GOD AT WORK

I thank my God every time I remember you, constantly praying with joy in every one of my prayers for all of you, because of your sharing in the gospel from the first day until now. I am confident of this, that the one who began a good work among you will bring it to completion by the day of Jesus Christ. (Philippians 1:3-6)

Growing up in Zimbabwe, whenever we came across a roadworks sign on the side of the road, it was always somewhat of an ironic statement. There was the sign – a metal triangle with a red border around its edges. Its white centre displaying a silhouette of a person industriously digging with a shovel. The Highway Code informed you that this road sign means 'men at work'. However, the reality of the situation was always quite different.

Seeing a road sign like this did not necessarily mean you were about to encounter anyone on the road ahead. Most often these 'men at work' were invisible. But, on the rare occasion when you were rewarded with a rare sighting of these elusive people, there would always be a group of them. Now, to be fair, there would usually be one person who would be doing something that looked like work – and yes, usually digging something on the road with a shovel. So far so good. However, all his colleagues would be standing around him watching. Or they would be in a group standing around a hurriedly made fire on the side of the road boiling a kettle to make a cup of tea. Somehow the triangular road sign had not captured this more relaxed attitude that came with being a 'man at work'.

This light-hearted story sits in stark contrast to what Paul is talking about in today's passage.

Here we see Paul again praying for other believers. For their spiritual growth and relationship with Jesus. He says that he prays for them with joy because he knows that God is at work in their lives.

God is at work! He is not sitting on the side-lines and watching or laughing when we trip up or looking away when we fall. No. He is involved. He is at work within us, and He will continue to work until the job of transforming our lives is complete. He is even at work within us as we pray, changing us. Helping us to pray according to his will and not our own.

Prayer is powerful and valuable and can be effective in the spiritual realms to bring about victory. But we need to always remember that it is not the prayer itself that is activating some magical power – it is God who is at work. It is God who is acting and moving and doing.

Paul is full of joy because he is witnessing God working within the lives of his friends. Transforming them and changing them. Making them more like Jesus. This is something to celebrate.

I've always smiled to myself and thought that everyone in church should be issued with a T-shirt that has a picture of one of those triangular road signs and the words 'God at work' printed on it. This would remind us as well as let everyone else know that we are all work-in-progress. God is still digging away within us. We are being transformed into the likeness of Jesus, but it takes time and will not be complete until the day of Christ's return.

So, when we pray, let us also give thanks for those whom we are partnered with in the gospel. Those whom we are walking this journey of discipleship with. Rejoicing when we recognise God at work in them as well as within our own lives, safe in the knowledge that God won't leave the job unfinished.

Jesus, thank you that you are actively at work in my life and in the lives of my friends. It's wonderful to know that I don't have to walk this road alone, that you are always there for me. I trust that you know what is best for me and I ask you to please continue changing me to become more like you.
Amen.

DAY 22 – PEACE THROUGH PRAYER

Do not worry about anything, but in everything by prayer and supplication with thanksgiving let your requests be made known to God. And the peace of God, which surpasses all understanding, will guard your hearts and your minds in Christ Jesus. (Philippians 4:6-7)

Some years ago, I was diagnosed with cancer (Non-Hodgkin's Lymphoma). In the early days of my diagnosis, the doctors wanted to take a wait-and-see approach as the type of cancer I had was what they referred to as a 'slow grower', so they were not in a rush to give treatment at that time.

I remember my mother was particularly anxious and wanted to know why they simply didn't just 'chop it out'. Later we learned that this type of cancer can't be removed surgically as it is part of the lymphatic system and they preferred to wait until treatment was necessary due to danger of death, before treating. This is quite possibly due to rules around the free healthcare available to citizens in the UK, I'm not sure. (Read the full story in my book 'Standing in the Storm: Living with Faith and Cancer' 2022, Instant Apostle).

What I want you to learn from this is that when faced with a medical problem, our instant reaction is to seek a cure. A treatment. A medicine. Something to help remove the infection or to ease the pain. I must admit whenever I get a headache, I quickly reach for the paracetamol.

So, what do we do when we begin to worry or get anxious?

Stress and anxiety seem to be growing in society today. It is good that mental health problems such as these are being addressed more openly and that treatments are available.

It's amazing that thousands of years ago, Paul also addresses the problem of worry in his letter to the Philippians. Anxiety is nothing new.

When we start to fear, we should firstly turn to prayer. Prayer is part of the remedy for worry, as well as sharing our concerns with a trusted friend.

In every situation that causes us to be afraid or to worry about the unknown, Paul instructs us to pray about it. To bring the situation to God.

It is interesting that Paul encourages us to also include thanksgiving into the mix when praying about our worries. This helps to shift our perspective to see more of the positives in the situation. By giving thanks first, we are reminding ourselves of the good things God has already done for us. Then in the light of this, we can tell him about our worries – trusting that as he has helped in the past, so He will be faithful to help again.

The peace of God is an amazingly powerful thing. All during my journey through cancer I was praying and bringing my worries to Jesus. It reached a point where I was at peace with the situation. God filled me with His supernatural peace to such a point where I was calm and relaxed. I was convinced that He was in control of my situation, even if it meant I would die. I was at peace, and this helped me enormously through a very difficult time.

We can all ask God to give us His peace that surpasses all human understanding, so that it fills us completely. And as it does, it will guard our hearts and fill our minds so that fear does not get a grip on us – as we keep our eyes firmly fixed on Jesus.

Today, if we are facing situations that are causing us to worry, let's turn to God in prayer and tell Him about it. And then allow Him to fill us with his amazing peace.

Jesus, I bring my fears and worries to you today. Help me to trust you. Please remind me that You are in control of my life and not me. Thank you that you are faithful and kind. That you are victorious and are seated on the throne in heaven. Please fill me with your peace so that my worries dissolve away and trouble me no more.
Amen.

FURTHER READING & QUESTIONS 4

PHILIPPIANS 1-2

Wider Reading – Prayer

Pray in the Spirit - Ephesians 6:18

God hears our Prayers - Jeremiah 29:11-14

According to God's Will - 1 John 5:14-15

Humble Yourselves - 2 Chronicles 7:14

Powerful and Effective - James 5:13-16

Pray for your Enemies - Matthew 5:43-48

Be Faithful in Prayer - Romans 12:12

Pray Like This - Matthew 6:9-13

Discussion Questions - Prayer

What is prayer?

Why is prayer so important?

How often do you pray BIG prayers? What can you do to pray BIG prayers more often?

Using a percentage – give an estimate as to how much of your prayer time is for your own needs.

Now do the same and estimate how much of your prayer time is for the needs of others?

How much time do you devote to simply listening to hear from Jesus?

Does anything need to change?

Can you give an example of a time when God has answered your prayer (big or small)?

Make a note of these so that you can give thanks for them. They can remind you of God's faithfulness in the future.

PART V

LIVING FOR JESUS

DAY 23 – PUT ON YOUR NEW SELF

You were taught to put away your former way of life, your old self, corrupt and deluded by its lusts, and to be renewed in the spirit of your minds, and to clothe yourselves with the new self, created according to the likeness of God in true righteousness and holiness. (Ephesians 4:22-24)

The other day, my wife encouraged me to throw out a pair of old walking boots that had come to the end of their usefulness. The soles had holes in them, allowing water to seep into my socks whenever I stepped into a puddle. One of the shoelaces had snapped a bit off one end, so tying up the right hand shoe was tricky. A couple of the fastenings that you wrap the shoelace around to hold it in place higher up the shoe had either bent or snapped off. It was time for them to be replaced.

I don't like throwing things away, especially if they could still prove useful one day. But as space is limited, this is something I have had to learn to do – although there are times that I still find it hard.

Besides, I had bought a new pair of shoes and was now wearing those instead. I had to throw the old pair out.

In today's passage, Paul is encouraging the Ephesian Christians to throw away their old way of living as they have already exchanged it for a new one when they came to know about Jesus and chose to follow Him.

The old self includes: greed; selfishness; thought patterns that do not fit with the teachings of Jesus; greed; foolish talking; sexual immorality; following ones own desires; telling lies; stealing (see Ephesians 4:17-5:20) – the list could go on, but I'm sure you get the idea.

Paul explains that there are elements of some of these traits within everyone's lifestyle before they met Jesus. In essence – we are all tainted by sin.

It is interesting to note that Paul says we need to 'put off' this old self. Like a pair of broken and useless walking boots, sometimes we keep it hanging around. Maybe on the odd occasion we decide that the old boots are more comfortable or familiar than the new ones, and we put them on again for a bit. Perhaps it is difficult to throw things away – we may have enjoyed some of the aspects of wearing those old useless shoes.

Taking something off is a choice, just as putting something else new on is. We need to choose to take off our old way of doing things, our old life, our before-Jesus lifestyle and we need to choose to put on our new self, our new way of thinking, of being, and doing which is centred on Jesus and His righteousness and holiness.

Our old way of living no longer fits with this new way in Christ. Running back to certain things we may find difficult to let go of every so often is not what Jesus intends for us.

Putting on the new pair of shoes was interesting. I knew it was the right thing to do. I liked them as I had chosen to buy them, and I was pleased with my choice. However, at first, they didn't feel as comfortable as my old shoes did. After wearing them for a while I got blisters on my heels and started longing for my old boots again. But they looked good, had fully functioning shoelaces, were watertight and did a great job.

Starting a new relationship with Jesus, or with anyone, can be difficult for a while. There will be times of challenge where something rubs against us and causes a blister, so an adjustment is needed. We may want to turn away from Jesus and take the easier path, but we would be giving up the new life that He gives if we do. Besides, a few weeks later the new boots were feeling very comfortable, even more so than the old pair.

There may be aspects of our 'old selves' that keep making the odd appearance in our lives. Let us choose to 'put them off' and give them to Jesus today.

Jesus, help me to live according to your will. There are times when my old self seems to creep back onto me – help me to take it off and to choose to put on my new self again, life that is centred on you and your holiness. Change my heart and my mind to be more like You.
Amen.

DAY 24 – BE HUMBLE

Do nothing from selfish ambition or conceit, but in humility regard others as better than yourselves. Let each of you look not to your own interests, but to the interests of others. (Philippians 2:3-4)

Being humble is an attitude of the heart, where one has a modest opinion of one's own importance.

This is different to believing that we have no importance at all. True humility is the ability to keep our egos in check and to accept that often, we are not the smartest or most talented people in the room.

However, when our contributions and talents are recognised and genuine praise is given, it is not prideful to accept that praise in a measured way.

For me, the key to being humble is given in today's passage. We are to value others above ourselves. It is all about others.

Humility is often associated with how much pride a person appears to have or does not have. Now on one level, this is true. However, I think humility reaches further than this.

Humility is a behaviour that puts the needs and interests of others before our own. It does not neglect our own needs, but rather sees the needs of others as having a higher priority.

So, humility can be seen in the church where the church leader is happy to also make the coffee or put out the chairs as well as to preach. It can be seen in how we treat the elderly person or someone with a mental illness. It can be seen in how we include children in the worship life of the church, rejoicing in it and not criticising or enduring it, but taking part with willingness and love for their sake. It is preferring others by being willing to sing songs that are not our favourites or sitting in a chair that is not completely to our liking so that someone else is able to sit in the spot that is best for them.

When everyone starts to get the ideas that preferring the other is what Jesus is asking each of us to do, it benefits everyone.

If everyone is making a determined effort to prefer each other, it means that you will be the recipient of someone else' preferential treatment. However, this should not be our goal. Living in the way Jesus has called us to live is what we are aiming to do, with or without the added benefit of someone preferring us in return.

Jesus' life is one that shows true humility. He chose to prefer us by laying aside his majesty and by becoming human (Philippians 2:7). He came to be a servant, not a king (Luke 22:27). He came to do the will of God, not His own (John 6:38). He gave up His life so that we may be saved from our sin (Philippians 2:8).

Humility is often not easy. It demands we make a conscious decision, to choose ourselves or to choose the other person instead.

In this passage, Paul was speaking about humility as part of the wider context of encouraging unity amongst Christian in the church of Philippi. Indeed, humility is required for unity to be achieved but humility is not merely a practical tool in a unity-making machine, it is living our lives with the mindset of Christ.[1]

Let us make a determined effort to prefer the needs and interests of others above our own today.

Jesus, help me to prefer the needs of others today. To lay down my way of doing things to help someone else reach their potential; to put aside my preferred tastes for the benefit of someone else. Create a humble heart in me Jesus, just as you showed me what a life of true humility looks like. Help me to be more like you, Jesus.
Amen.

DAY 25 – SPEAK WELL

Let no evil talk come out of your mouths, but only what is useful for building up, as there is need, so that your words may give grace to those who hear. (Ephesians 4:29)

Some years ago, the church I attend went through a difficult time. There were a couple of people in the church who were unhappy with the leadership and started to gossip about things. They whispered in the ears of anyone who would listen and began to influence the hearts and minds of a significant number of people within the church. They did not speak to the leadership about their problems or concerns, but rather decided to grumble and complain to others about things instead.

This began to stir up trouble and eventually came to a head when some very angry people made the decision to leave the church.

It was very sad and very painful for everyone – even those not involved in the confrontation.

I usually don't like sharing negative stories, but I hope that a lesson can be learned here. If we have a problem with someone, whoever they may be, we should be brave enough to actually speak with them about it before things have a chance to get worse.

If we decide to push those feelings down and try to ignore the problem, or decide to gossip about them instead, a lot of pain and upset will result. Gossip is never a good thing. Half-truths and misinformation can be spread to the cost and pain of the person being spoken about. Gossip tears down and destroys.

As Christians we are called to speak well of people, to build up and encourage them. We may not agree with everything someone says but this can be talked about in a calm and sensible way face to face.

Here, Paul instructs the Ephesians to avoid gossip and hurtful talk, but to rather focus on using their words wisely to encourage and to build up others. Words can also bring clarity, correction, and healing as part of the building up process. He encourages them to be careful with the words they employ and to use them well with the ultimate goal of being of benefit to the hearer in mind.

This is good advice for us too.

We live in a culture where gossip is celebrated. There are entire publications devoted to spreading half-truths or sometimes downright lies about people who are usually famous for something or other. Airing dirty laundry may sell magazines and newspapers, but these issues are not for public consumption and should be correctly dealt with in private.

Proverbs 18:21 reminds us how powerful the words we speak can be: "Death and life are in the power of the tongue, and those who love it will eat its fruits."

It is easy to gossip and to criticise. Negativity comes easily. It is up to us to decide each day to 'put on our new self' and choose not to speak badly of others, or indeed read things that are doing this.

How can we encourage and build up those we meet today? Will what we say be of benefit to them?

If not, it may be better for us to remain silent, or better still to arrange to have a conversation were the problems we have can be discussed honestly and openly.

Speak well.

Jesus, help me to speak well of others. Help me to recognise when I am engaging in gossip and am not saying things that will encourage or build up those around me. May my words be for the benefit of others – let this be my motivation for the words I speak today.
Amen.

DAY 26 – BE KIND

Be kind to one another, tender-hearted, forgiving one another, as God in Christ has forgiven you. (Ephesians 4:32)

It amazes me how kind children can be.

My eldest daughter does not like eating chewy sweets, which rules out quite an array of options. When someone at her school has a birthday, they sometimes bring in small packets of these chewy sweets to give to their classmates. Each time, instead of ripping open the packet and eating all the sweets as soon as she crosses the threshold of the school gates, like many others do, she keeps her packet in her pocket and gives it to her sister who loves those type of sweets.

On another occasion, there was a raffle at school to raise money for a cancer charity. There were a lot of prizes, and the drawing of the tickets took a long time. It ended up that my daughter won two prizes which she was very pleased about. When all the prizes had been given out, one of her friends was a little bit upset that she had not won anything. With a big and generous heart, my daughter gave her friend the cuddly toy she had just won so that her friend wouldn't feel left out.

There is nothing we can ever do to earn our salvation. It is a free gift full of grace and mercy from a generous God. We are saved by grace and grace alone, not by doing good deeds or being kind. The truth of this is not lost on me, however, there was a time when my view of things got a little distorted. The problem was, I was only looking at things from one angle. The idea that doing good works will not earn you salvation morphed into a more subtle subconscious thought that 'good people can't be saved' because salvation is not based on how 'good' we are. However, a wiser Christian whom I respect greatly pointed out to me that although salvation cannot be earned, it was *for* good works that we have been saved. Being a good person, acting justly and doing good things is a result of the saving work of Christ working within us to transform us to become more like Christ. So good people can be saved, and even those who were not so good to begin with, will become good once the grace and love of God is within them.

Paul's simple exhortation to the Ephesian Christians in this letter is to be kind. It is interesting to notice that the focus of Paul's instruction here is quite narrow. He is telling Christians to be kind to other Christians, to show compassion and love to fellow believers in the context of promoting church unity – although I am convinced this instruction of 'be kind' can and should reach beyond our church walls to impact the world and people around us too. Elsewhere in the Bible we are clearly encouraged to love everyone, to act justly and help others whether they are Christians or not.

Forgiveness is a key element of kindness. Paul teaches us here, that forgiveness is of fundamental importance to Christians because it is the very thing that Jesus gave his life for. He literally died so that forgiveness could be offered to us. Without Jesus's death, there would be no forgiveness of sin. It is because of God's kindness that He chose to lay aside His majesty, become part of His creation, so that He might pay the penalty for our sin in our place and thereby restore our relationship with Himself.

So, it follows that if we want to be Christians – to live for Jesus – we also need to forgive. And forgiveness allows healing to begin.

If we were to rate ourselves on a 'kindness meter' by giving ourselves a mark out of ten, what score would we get?

Whatever the answer, I think there is still some growing to be done inside each of us as we continue to choose to put on our new selves and become more mature in Christ.

How easy do we find it to forgive others? Perhaps there is someone in our lives right now whom we are struggling to forgive. Maybe now is a good time to begin by bringing the person and the situation before God in prayer?

As Jesus told His disciples to become more like children so that they could enter the Kingdom of heaven (Matthew 18:1-5), let us follow the children's example and show unconditional kindness to those we meet today.

Jesus, help me to be kind. To show love and compassion to fellow Christians as well as to those outside the church. Help me to forgive, just as you have forgiven me. Today I want to bring before you.... You know them and you know me. You are aware of the situation, the pain and the conflict. Today, I choose to forgive and release them from what they did/said. Help me to continue to forgive in the days and weeks to come.
Amen.

DAY 27 – CHILDREN OF LIGHT

For once you were darkness, but now in the Lord you are light. Live as children of light— for the fruit of the light is found in all that is good and right and true. Try to find out what is pleasing to the Lord. Take no part in the unfruitful works of darkness, but instead expose them. For it is shameful even to mention what such people do secretly; but everything exposed by the light becomes visible, for everything that becomes visible is light. (Ephesians 5:8-13)

In some church settings, candles are used regularly as part of worship. Visual symbols, such as a candle, can help to illustrate powerful spiritual truths in a practical way.

During Lent, some churches light special Lenten candles as part of the service. There are six candles in total – one for each Sunday of Lent. On the first Sunday, all the candles are lit and then one is extinguished during the service. The following Sunday five are lit and another extinguished and so on until on Good Friday. Here the death of Jesus is remembered, and the final candle left alight, which

symbolises Christ and is often a different colour to the rest, is
extinguished leaving only darkness.

On Easter Sunday, the Candle representing Jesus is lit again,
symbolising his resurrection from the dead – his light shines for all
the world to see, piercing the darkness. Jesus' victory over sin and
death is no match for the darkness of the world.

I have heard it said that darkness is nothing more than the
absence of light. Where there is light, darkness cannot exist. A tiny
sparkle of light is enough to make a room not completely dark
anymore. Increase the amount of light and the shadows created
become less obvious and the light shines more brightly enabling you
to see more clearly. But even a single flickering flame of a candle is
enough to push back the darkness because light is the dominant force.
There cannot be darkness in the spot where light is present.

As followers of Jesus, our spirits are rejuvenated within us and
we are also supposed to be filled with the person of the Holy Spirit.
We are Jesus-carriers. Wherever we place our feet, we take the
kingdom of God with us. We are His ambassadors. We carry the light
of Christ within us, shining out for all to see.

Paul also puts it this way in his letter to the Philippians: "Do all
things without murmuring and arguing, so that you may be blameless
and innocent, children of God without blemish in the midst of a
crooked and perverse generation, in which you shine like stars in the
world." (Philippians 2: 14-15).

As we start to live our lives God's way, as we allow the Holy
Spirit to transform our thoughts and our behaviour, we begin to shine
like the stars into the darkness and brokenness of the world
around us.

If this is the case, we should therefore have nothing to do with
things of darkness. We need to get rid of those things in our lives that
are sinful and are against the life Jesus gives to us.

Paul encourages the Ephesian Christians, and indeed he
encourages us, to expose the sin that may still be lingering with us.
We do this by confessing our sin to God and to trusted Christians

around us who can help and support us as we work together to take off our old selves and put on our new selves in Christ every day.

Being accountable to a fellow believer can really help with this.

Perhaps there are dark corners still lingering within our lives today – parts of our lives that we have not yet fully surrendered to Jesus?

Today, let us take the first step of repenting of our sin. Turning away and asking Jesus to change our hearts and our minds to be like His own. And as we do so, let us ask the Holy Spirit to fill us so that the light of Christ will shine more brightly within us and be seen by all around us.

Jesus, you are the light of the world. There is no darkness so powerful that it can overcome your light. Help me to shine for you so that your light within me will touch and affect those around me. Jesus, I am sorry for the things of darkness that I still hold on to, those things that I know are not pleasing to you. Jesus, please forgive me. I decide to turn away from them today and ask you to renew my mind and change my heart and behaviour. Holy Spirit, fill me and help me to shine more brightly for Jesus.
Amen.

DAY 28 – LIVE FOR JESUS

And whatever you do, in word or deed, do everything in the name of
the Lord Jesus, giving thanks to God the Father through him.
(Colossians 3:17)

William Wilberforce was a British Member of Parliament in the late
eighteenth century and is famous for his instrumental part in helping
to abolish the international trade in slaves. Shortly after becoming an
MP in 1784 he became an evangelical Christian. This led to a crisis
of conscience for William as he desperately wanted to serve God and
was therefore contemplating leaving politics in order to do this.

It was his friend and spiritual mentor, John Newton (who
famously wrote the hymn 'Amazing Grace') who encouraged him to
stay in politics as this too was an area where he could serve and
worship God, in and through his work.[1]

Sometimes we can fall into the trap of thinking that we can only
serve God and be effective for His kingdom if we 'work for the
church' as a priest, or worship leader or evangelist etc. It is easy not to

recognise that whatever we do, if we work as if we are doing so for Jesus, we can have an impact for His kingdom where we are.

This means anyone and everyone can live for Jesus, right where they are, and have significance and make an impact.

Farmers, lawyers, street sweepers, ice-cream van drivers, postal workers, teachers, supermarket checkout operators, students, children, web designers, doctors, mothers, fathers, retired people, actors, authors, financial advisors, mobile phone repairers, butchers, factory workers and bakers – everyone can live for Jesus right where they are.

When we make the decision to follow Jesus, the priorities of our lives change radically forever. We are no longer living for ourselves, but for Him. We are no longer the ones in the driving seat of our lives and our destinies, Jesus is. The primary purpose of our lives becomes an echo of the words of Jesus "yet, not my will but yours be done." (Luke 22:42).

We are to live for God.

We don't have to get a fancy theological degree or wear some special outfit to do this. We simply need to listen and obey. We can live lives for Jesus wherever we may be, and as we do so, we are to shine the light of Christ that is glowing within us so that those around us may see the reason for the hope we have.

What have I got in my hand? What am I already able to do? Where am I already placed? Who do I already have contact with? – answering these questions will help to position us to be ready to serve Jesus and live for Him wherever we may be. We will be able to identify opportunities to talk about Jesus more easily and maybe, just maybe, we will be able to start to see the various roles we play in life as being an important part of the growth of the Kingdom of God – because they are.

Let us pause for a moment and allow Paul's words to speak deeply to us. Read the passage through slowly. Then read it again out loud, pausing at every comma allowing the Holy Spirit to speak to you. Finally read it through for a third time, pausing to add your own words of prayer at each pause:

"whatever you do, in word or deed, do everything in the name of the Lord Jesus, giving thanks to God the Father through him" (Colossians 3:17)

Jesus, help me to live for you. Show me where you want me to be and what you want me to be doing. Help me to use what is already in my hand to serve and honour you, right where I am.
Amen.

FURTHER READING &
QUESTIONS 5

PHILIPPIANS 3-4

Wider Reading – Living for Jesus

Renew your mind - Romans 12:1-2

Love in Action - Romans 12:9-21

Keep in Step with the Spirit - Galatians 5:22-26

God of compassion - Psalm 103

Gossip - Proverbs 18:6-8, 18:21

Power of our words - James 3:3-6

Confess - 1 John 1:9

Forgiveness - Psalm 103-12

A City on a Hill - Matthew 5:14-16

Discussion Questions – Living for Jesus

Why is it important to recognise that although we are saved by grace, we need to continue being aware of our potential for sinfulness?

If we are honest with ourselves, many of the things we are asked to do (and not do) to live for Jesus are incredibly difficult, or impossible to do. Why do you think this is?

What practical things can you do to 'prefer others' either at home or at church?

How do you identify gossip? When you do, what strategies do you use to stop the gossiping conversation?

What have you already got in your hand – or in other words, where are you already placed or what are you already able to do that you could see as an opportunity for you to live for Jesus?

After looking at this week's topic, are there any areas in your life that you feel need improvement for you to live for Jesus more effectively?

PART VI

SUFFERING

DAY 29 – PAUL IN CHAINS

I want you to know, beloved, that what has happened to me has actually helped to spread the gospel, so that it has become known throughout the whole imperial guard and to everyone else that my imprisonment is for Christ; and most of the brothers and sisters, having been made confident in the Lord by my imprisonment, dare to speak the word with greater boldness and without fear. (Philippians 1:12-14)

Some years ago, on a visit to Cape Town, South Africa I visited the notorious Robben Island. Located just off the coast of the city in Table Bay it was used as a prison for political prisoners during the apartheid era. Several well-known political prisoners were held there over the years including Nelson Mandela.

Our tour group was led by a former prisoner. He spoke about what life was like as a prisoner and how unpleasant it was. How the seemingly pointless manual labour of moving piles of big rocks from one place to another and back again, by hand, could physically break a man. How the severe constraint of liberty could take its toll. How the conditions they had to endure made their imprisonment even more unbearable.

However, the imprisonment of political activists such as Nelson Mandela alongside many others, drew the attention of the world to the prejudice and injustice of racial segregation that was going on in the country.

After many years, things finally started to turn a corner. On 11th February 1990[1] Nelson Mandela was released from prison after 27 years. He then led his political party's negotiations with the ruling party to bring an end to apartheid. In 1994, South Africa held its first free and fair elections and Mandela was elected as South African president.

In a similar way, Paul's imprisonment had served to highlight and advance the gospel. Like the political prisoners who were locked up to stop their resistance and ideology from spreading, their imprisonment helped it to spread. Paul was imprisoned because he was preaching the gospel. Rather than stifling it, his imprisonment caused the gospel to spread even more – soldiers in the palace guard were hearing the gospel and some had even become Christians as a result (see Philippians 4:22).

Not only was the gospel spreading despite Paul's imprisonment, but the fact that he was suffering for the gospel also served to embolden other believers. They could see the example Paul was setting and were inspired to also proclaim the gospel without fear, just as he had done.

Times of suffering are unpleasant. They are times we would prefer to avoid. No one likes to suffer. But we can't escape from the reality that life can get hard, ugly and painful. We live in a broken and hurting world and we can get broken and hurt along the journey of life.

But all is not lost.

Our times of suffering can mean something that reaches far beyond the immediate pain and difficulties.

On day 28, we explored how we can live for Jesus wherever we are and whatever we are doing. Let's apply this to suffering. Yes, even in our times of suffering, we can choose to live for Jesus as Paul shows us here. We can choose to face suffering and death with the courage, hope and integrity that Jesus gives us, despite the pain. And just as what happened for Paul and for those South African prisoners, you never know how far and wide the message of the gospel of Jesus at work in your life will be heard - even within the suffering.

Let us not be afraid of suffering, but rather let us prepare ourselves by holding on to Jesus more tightly so that when times of suffering come, we are ready, and we can move forward confidently without fear because we know God is at work.

Jesus, help me to remember that when I encounter times of suffering and pain, that you are still at work. Help me to continue to live for you even when things get difficult so that your work in my life will be seen more clearly and heard more powerfully by those around me.
Amen.

DAY 30 – NOT ALONE

Epaphras, my fellow-prisoner in Christ Jesus, sends greetings to you, and so do Mark, Aristarchus, Demas, and Luke, my fellow-workers. (Philemon 23-24)

Some nights, the quietness and calm of the darkness is harshly interrupted by shrieks and screams. I force myself to open my heavy eyes and drag myself out of bed into the cold night air. Half stumbling and half shuffling I make my way across the landing towards my five year old daughter's room.

Often, I find her sat upright in the middle of her bed with streams of tears pouring down her face. Still screaming and crying.

A nightmare.

I talk gently to her, reassuring her that she was only dreaming. I often stroke her hair and hold her tight, hoping that my presence and embrace will help to reassure and calm her, helping her to feel safe and loved.

Often the night light needs to be switched on for her to be able to fall asleep again.

When we face dark times in our lives, how often do we shout out? We long for someone else to be there with us, to reassure and comfort us.

In this seemingly insignificant passage from Paul's letter to Philemon, we get an insight into his situation as he is in prison for sharing the gospel. Epaphras is also in prison with Paul. I would suggest that as he is named in this pastoral letter, he is also a fellow believer, as are Mark, Aristarchus, Demas and Luke. They aren't in prison but help to continue the work of the church and because of this, would visit Paul often.

I love this passage because it shows us that Paul is not alone! In this very dark and difficult time of being imprisoned, he has company in his suffering.

Looking back at the previous chapters about family and unity, it should come as no surprise that Paul is not abandoned to suffer on his own. These people are living examples of what it means to be the family of God and how we should be living our lives together by supporting and helping each other.

Hopefully, when we encounter difficulties and trials, we have a network of Christian friends – a spiritual family – whom we can call and rely upon for help and support. If not, perhaps this is something to be prayed about and worked towards.

But even if we do find ourselves alone in our suffering, or indeed we may feel alone even if there are others around us, let us remember that this is not actually the case - we are not alone. As a believer in Jesus, we can never be alone no matter what is happening around us.

God has promised us that he will never abandon or disown us (Deuteronomy 31:8). He is right there in the midst of the suffering with us. He is there to help us, to fight for us and to comfort us. His light shines in the darkness – the best nightlight you could ever have.

There is always hope.

Jesus is the source of Christian hope, and this hope is certain and secure. So even when things get difficult, we may be feeling the pressure all around us, but we won't be crushed. We may feel worried and anxious, but we don't need to lose hope. We may be persecuted and mistreated, but we are not abandoned. We may be beaten up or knocked out, but we are not destroyed – because Jesus is with us, and we can stand secure in Him. (2 Corinthians 4:8-9).

So, when we find ourselves in times of trouble, remember to turn to Jesus because we will find Him right there by our side in the middle of the storm.

We are not alone.

Jesus, thank you that you are always with me. You will never abandon me. Thank you that you hold me closer to you when I am in the midst of difficulties and suffering. Help me to know that you are there. Help me to praise You in the storm.

Amen.

DAY 31 – GIFT OF SUFFERING

For he has graciously granted you the privilege not only of believing in Christ, but of suffering for him as well— since you are having the same struggle that you saw I had and now hear that I still have. (Philippians 1:29-30)

My two year old son loves to receive gifts. I think he enjoys unwrapping the present more than the actual gift itself. In fact, it is quite difficult to keep him from unwrapping other people's gifts at birthday parties. He is just so enthusiastic about tearing that paper off to discover what is hidden underneath.

I would imagine most of us can identify with this eagerness to unwrap a gift because we have a desire to see what lies within the paper and ribbon. So, it may be strange to speak of suffering as being a 'gift'.

Gifts are usually good and pleasant. They are often things we were wanting, although sometimes not. The gift is given with good intention by the giver – a desire to bless and celebrate.

Let's be real for a moment. Suffering is not nice. We don't choose to suffer and would much rather avoid it. It is painful and costly and unwanted.

But sometimes, God allows suffering in our lives. We live in a broken and fallen world, so there will be pain and suffering within our life experience.

We often pray and ask God to deliver us *from* suffering and sometimes our request is granted.

However, what about those times when God does not deliver us from it, and we find ourselves right in the middle of it? Does this mean God no longer loves us or has abandoned us? Does it mean our faith is not good enough, or we are somehow being punished?

No.

Suffering is part of the normal Christian experience. It is part of the package.

Here Paul explains that suffering plays a part in the Christian life. He says that not only were the Philippian Christians blessed to believe in Jesus, but they were also blessed because they were allowed to suffer for Jesus too. Later in the letter (Philippians 3:10-11) he explains that his desire to know Christ more deeply and intimately means that he too will suffer, because Jesus suffered. He can only become more like-Christ as he experiences the things Christ experienced and live the life Christ lived. So, times of suffering help him to move closer to Christ-likeness, which is the aim of our discipleship.

God allows us to go through times of suffering because sometimes God wants to deliver us *through* it. There is much to learn about God and about ourselves as we go through times of suffering. It helps to refine and to strengthen our faith and draws us closer to Jesus.

We don't need to go looking for opportunities where we can subject ourselves to suffering. That would be wrong. But when times of suffering come to us, we should view them differently – as gifts and opportunities for us to grow in our discipleship.

Jesus, help me to see my personal suffering differently. If your will is for me to go through times of suffering, help me to be ready. To be standing on a solid foundation of faith in you, so that when the storm comes, I will be able to stand. No one likes to suffer, Jesus, and I pray that you help those who are suffering now. Help them to trust in you and may you bring them safely out the other side soon.

Amen.

DAY 32 – FEARLESS GOSPEL

Pray also for me, so that when I speak, a message may be given to me to make known with boldness the mystery of the gospel, for which I am an ambassador in chains. Pray that I may declare it boldly, as I must speak. (Ephesians 6:19-20)

It was a cold winter's morning when my sister-in-law and I were shopping at our local supermarket. Our grocery shopping done, we decided to stop for a drink in the coffee shop that was strategically situated just after the checkout isles.

We were sitting at a table in the comfortably padded chairs sipping our drinks, when I felt the Holy Spirit give me a nudge. I had noticed one of the baristas, who had just served us, had a cast on her arm. In that moment I got a very strong feeling that the Holy Spirit wanted to work through me to speak to this person. I have learnt not to ignore strong feelings like this – but I was terrified!

What if she refused to listen? What if she thought I was mad? What if the things I thought the Holy Spirit wanted to say to her were wrong? What if I was just making it all up?

I could have listened to all these fears and reasons I was quickly giving myself for not following the prompting of the Holy Spirit, but the urgency in my spirit did not dissipate, it increased.

So, I took a deep breath and walked up to the serving area.

At that moment the barista with the cast on her arm was taking a break around the back in the kitchen. I took my chance and stood at the kitchen entrance, explained I was a Christian and told her that I thought Jesus wanted to tell her something. I then delivered the message and she thanked me.

That was it.

I don't know what happened to her as I never saw her again despite returning to the same coffee shop many times since. I hope and pray God used that encounter for His glory. I may have looked like an idiot, but I overcame my fears and chose to be brave and obey the prompting and leading of the Holy Spirit despite my fear.

In his letter to the Ephesian church, Paul shows vulnerability. He admits that he is afraid – why would you ask for prayer to help you be fearless if you were without fear? He is also humble enough to ask for prayer from others despite his leadership position.

Again, he points out that he is in chains, imprisoned and suffering for his faith. Yet despite these difficult and painful circumstances, he is determined to continue with the task that Jesus has given him – the very thing that caused this hardship in the first place – declaring the gospel.

Doing so could cause further misery, but Paul asks for courage so that he can continue to share the good news of Jesus despite his fear and the possible consequences.

When we face hardships, we too should pray and ask others to pray for us, so that we may be able to continue to further the work of the Kingdom despite the suffering or pain it may cause us personally.

We need to be fearless people of Christ. Unashamed of the gospel for it is life and liberty for those who hear and believe.

It can be a challenge to let those in our workplace know that we are Christians. We may risk isolation or persecution. But we need to be like Paul and continue to live for Jesus and let others know that we are doing so, even if it makes us afraid.

Jesus, help me to live for You where I work and where I play. I understand that being a Christian is not just something I do on a Sunday, but something I choose to do every day of my life. Help me to be brave when I feel afraid to share the goodness of the gospel with others.
Amen.

DAY 33 – TO LIVE IS CHRIST

It is my eager expectation and hope that I will not be put to shame in any way, but that by my speaking with all boldness, Christ will be exalted now as always in my body, whether by life or by death. For to me, living is Christ and dying is gain. (Philippians 1:20-21)

This is one of the more famous passages found in Paul's letter to the Philippians that you may have seen printed on the side of a mug in the Christian bookshop or on a poster with a colourful sunset in the background. But what does it mean, and what does it teach us about suffering?

In the previous verse (vs. 19) Paul states that he is convinced that he will be delivered from his imprisonment because of the faithful and fervent prayers of the Philippian believers. But goes on to say that he needs courage so that Christ will be lifted up and honoured in his body, either through his life or his death.

He tells us that his preferred option would be death: "I am hard pressed between the two: my desire is to depart and be with Christ, for that is far better;" (Philippians 1:23) but he acknowledges that he is having difficulty in his decision because he knows that if he remains alive it will benefit the lives and faith of the believers in Philippi.

Death would mean a joyous union between him and Jesus. Living with Christ spiritually until the day when he would receive a new re-created body in the new heaven and the new earth. He would be free from sin and its effects, including suffering.

Because he knows his life is more valuable to be of service to his fellow believers at that moment, to help them grow in their faith, he is convinced that he will indeed live: "Since I am convinced of this, I know that I will remain and continue with all of you for your progress and joy in faith" (Philippians 1:25).

This means that he knows he will not die at that moment but will instead live.

He has already told us that 'to live is Christ' or in other words, to be alive as a Christian is to live a life like that of Jesus - who was rejected, suffered and died so that we might live.

Jesus himself tells his disciples what this life of service and dedication to Jesus will look like: "Then he said to them all, 'If any want to become my followers, let them deny themselves and take up their cross daily and follow me." (Luke 9:23).

We are called to deny our old nature by choosing to pick up our own metaphorical crosses every day, putting to death things that are not in line with the will of Jesus. We may have enjoyed or found pleasure in these things in the past and we may view our abstinence from them as suffering as we instead choose to do things Jesus' way.

Indeed, this way of living will also invariably move us to live countercultural lives. We will stand out because we are not doing or saying the same things that everyone else is.

It can be costly as we stand against the dominant currently held views of society, especially when those views that go directly against the Word of God are enshrined in the laws of the land. Problems and suffering will come because as Christians we are bound by a higher law – the law of God.

Choosing to live a life for Jesus includes suffering. Yet it is far better than living a life without Jesus.

He is there to help, comfort and guide us through the suffering. He can take something bad and recreate it into something new and beautiful. He can mend the cracks of our lives with gold and help us find splendour and meaning even when we are in the storms of life.

To live is Christ!

Jesus, help me to live for you. To live a life that reflects you in my choices and my attitudes. Help me to pick up my cross every day and to put your will above my own. Thank you that you have empowered me to live like this – I am not alone. I am not weak – with You I can do this!
Amen.

DAY 34 - THE PERSECUTED CHURCH

Devote yourselves to prayer, keeping alert in it with thanksgiving. At the same time pray for us as well that God will open to us a door for the word, that we may declare the mystery of Christ, for which I am in prison, so that I may reveal it clearly, as I should. Conduct yourselves wisely towards outsiders, making the most of the time. Let your speech always be gracious, seasoned with salt, so that you may know how you ought to answer everyone. (Colossians 4:2-6)

Thinking about suffering and persecution can make for uncomfortable reading. We don't like to be confronted with death or to deal with pain.

If you are like me, when a newsletter or prayer calendar from a Christian charity that works to support the persecuted Church arrives, it is very tempting to simply click 'delete' or pop it in the recycling bin. Avoiding confrontation may be easier and less uncomfortable, but is it the best thing for us to be doing?

This week, we have spent a lot of time looking at what we can learn about times of personal suffering from Paul's prison letters. But today, I think it would be useful for us to widen our perspective and give some thought to those who are part of the persecuted Church.

Open Doors is a leading charity in the UK who help persecuted believers around the world as well as encouraging the UK church to pray, give and speak for those who share our Christian faith, but not our freedom. Some statistics from their website[1] state that over 360 million Christians around the world suffer persecution and discrimination. This means that one in seven Christians around the world are persecuted for their faith.

Here in the west, we may not fully comprehend what it means to be persecuted for our faith in Jesus and what suffering this may cause. Yet, we can get some insight from Paul in his letter to the believers in Colossae.

Paul was being persecuted for his faith in Jesus. He had been put in prison in Rome because he had been sharing the gospel, the very 'mystery of Christ'.

I find it profoundly interesting that Paul's main request of his fellow believers, who are removed from his situation and are living far away, is for their prayer. Not for his deliverance from the situation, but for open doors for him to correctly represent Christ in spite of it, knowing full well that this could lead to further suffering as a consequence.

He also instructs them to act wisely towards those who don't share the faith. He encourages them not to reject such people, but instead to make the most of every opportunity to let the life and words of Jesus that are working and being expressed through their lives to be a witness to those around them. Not needlessly antagonising them, but rather being full of grace.

Ordinary Christians simply living out their faith and demonstrating Christ's teachings can be some of the most effective evangelists.

Today, let us remember our brothers and sisters in Christ who are being persecuted because of their faith. Let us share in their suffering because "If one member [of the body of Christ] suffers, all suffer together with it" (1 Corinthians 12:26 – words in brackets my own).

Let us do as Paul asked those believers in Colossae, to pray for them. To ask God to help them and most of all to provide them with open doors so that they may be able to continue to 'declare the mystery of Christ' even within their difficult and challenging situations.

Jesus, today I pray for my fellow brothers and sisters in Christ around the world who are suffering and being persecuted for their faith in you. I don't know their specific situations, but I ask that your presence will be with them. Help them to proclaim the mystery of Christ despite the difficulties they face – for your glory.
Amen.

FURTHER READING &
QUESTIONS 6

COLOSSIANS 1-2

Wider Reading – Suffering

We are Overcomers - 2 Corinthians 4:8-9

Suffering for Christ - Philippians 3:10-11

Paul's Many Sufferings - 2 Corinthians 11:23-29

The God of Comfort - 2 Corinthians 1:3-7

If One Part Suffers - 1 Corinthians 12:26

Pick Up your Cross - Matthew 16:24

Discussion Questions – Suffering

Who has inspired you in your faith, despite or because of their suffering?

Have you been encouraged or comforted by others in a time of trial or suffering? What effect did this have on you?

Is there someone you know who is going through a difficult time whom you could support or encourage right now?

How easy do you find it to see suffering as a gift? Why do you think this is?

Have you followed the prompting of the Holy Spirit in your life before? What happened?

How could you help others recognise when the Holy Spirit is prompting them to do something? Share some examples or advice.

Paul views death in a very positive way. How do you view death? Is it something you look forward to or something you fear? Why?

PART VII

HE IS RISEN

DAY 35 – DEATH ON A CROSS

And being found in human form,
    he humbled himself
    and became obedient to the point of death—
    even death on a cross.
    (Philippians 2:7-8)

You may have noticed that over the past six weeks, Jesus' death and resurrection kept creeping into other themes. You may have thought – why isn't he saving this until the end when we get closer to Easter?

This was no mistake – the death and resurrection of Jesus are so central to Christianity that everything else is influenced and informed by it.

Without it, we would not be adopted into God's family. We would be unable to forgive as He has forgiven us and therefore be unable to live in unity as the family of God in the way Jesus intends us to. We would not be living in the victory Jesus has already won for us, so wouldn't stand a chance in any form of spiritual warfare. Prayer would seem pointless and living in the way God wants us to live would be impossible, as we wouldn't have the indwelling presence and power of the Holy Spirit inside us to help and to guide us. And suffering would be unbearable as we would be without the hope that Jesus brings us – that light at the end of the dark tunnel that we can focus on that keeps us pressing forwards.

So here we are, starting week seven together, edging ever closer to celebrating Jesus' resurrection – His victory over sin and death.

But before we get there. We need to remember that Jesus died.

Today's verse is taken from a wider passage (Philippians 2:6-11) where Paul quotes what biblical scholars believe to be an early Christian hymn. This hymn beautifully explains the death and resurrection of Jesus.

It explains that Jesus was both fully God and fully human. He did not use His deity to side-step His purpose. Rather, in an act of pure humility and love, He was obedient. Even when this obedience led to His death on the cross.

Jesus died. Not because he wanted to die, but because He *had* to die to break the curse caused by sin that led to the separation between us and God.

We need to remember that Jesus did in fact die. He did not faint or fake it. Having a spear pushed into your heart through your lungs whilst hanging on a cross would certainty finish off anyone. And let's remember that the Roman soldiers who carried out the crucifixion were expert executioners.

One metaphor used to describe Jesus is that of a lamb. Jesus was crucified at Passover, the Jewish festival where they celebrate the angel of death 'passing over' their houses marked with the blood of a lamb as they prepared to escape from slavery in Egypt and then become the Israelite nation.

Here we see in Jesus, our sacrificial pure Passover lamb, slain that we may be 'passed over' by eternal death and separation from God. Jesus taking our place. Paying the price for our sin.

He had to die.

But why?

He died so that we might LIVE.

He died so that we could be forgiven[1], so that the brokenness of creation could start to be repaired. He died to enable God's Kingdom to begin to take back the ground lost to selfishness, greed and evil.

He died because God loves the world He created and wanted to rescue it, and us, from living in eternal punishment.

Jesus's death is good news for us.

It would be terribly sad if Jesus died and stayed that way. We would be grateful for his sacrifice, but there would be a deep sense of loss and guilt if He had stayed in the grave.

But the story does not end there. Jesus rose to life again on the third day - and this changes everything!

Jesus, thank you for your sacrifice. Thank you for dying for me so that I could be forgiven and live in right relationship with God. Thank you for the shame and the pain you endured on my behalf. Thank you for dying.
Amen.

DAY 36 – REDEMPTION AND FORGIVENESS

In him we have redemption through his blood, the forgiveness of our trespasses, according to the riches of his grace that he lavished on us. (Ephesians 1:7-8)

Redemption is one of those words that gets used quite a lot in Christian circles, yet it is easy to not fully grasp what the word means.

In fact, the word 'redemption' or the process of being 'redeemed' is not so alien in the financial world. You often see it on gift vouchers or website promotional codes.

In financial terms 'redemption' is used to describe the repayment of a debt on or before the date it was agreed for that dept to be paid in full.[1]

And this is what it means for Christians too.

The Bible tells us that we have all sinned (Romans 3:23) and that the cost of our sinfulness is death (Romans 6:23). Sin so altered creation that it broke our relationship with our holy God. Only the blood of a sacrifice that was pure and sinless could pay the death penalty demanded by our sinfulness.

Here we see Jesus, the only person in history who did not sin (1 John 3:5) offer Himself to be that sacrifice. He took our place and paid the price of our debt to God.

This redemption for our sin means that we can now be forgiven by God because the price demanded for it has been settled. The spiritual transaction has already taken place and it is God's desire to freely offer forgiveness to all who choose to ask for it.

I have already mentioned that I like to watch cop shows on TV.

One of the popular plot lines of these TV shows is kidnapping. After the criminals have kidnapped their victim, they usually demand a ransom from the worried family. This ransom is a demand for payment of a high price for the release of the person who is now in captivity.

Can you see the parallels between the kidnapped person and us?

We are held in captivity by the curse of sin and death until a high price is paid on our behalf for our release.

But Jesus has already paid that high price with his life when He died on the cross for us.

The prison door has been unlocked. We can leave at any time. Our ransom is paid. But so often we can believe that it is impossible to escape, or we think the door is still locked shut – so we stay where we are.

We may have never been told that we are actually in captivity as this is all we have ever known.

I want to tell you that there is more to life than the lonely, dreary prison cell that you may find yourself in today. There is fullness of life and joy available to you. There is true freedom and forgiveness waiting for you.

It begins with realising that the prison door has already been unlocked because your ransom has already been paid. You don't have to keep living a life with sin in it anymore.

Accept the gift freely offered by God through Jesus. Thank Him for dying for you and for forgiving you and decide to live your life for Him today.

Jesus, thank you for paying my price – for settling my debt – so that I can be forgiven. Help me to understand this wonderful gift of grace that you offer. I choose to live for you today, and every day – to walk in the forgiveness and freedom you give.
Amen.

DAY 37 – ALIVE IN CHRIST

And when you were dead in trespasses and the uncircumcision of your flesh, God made you alive together with him, when he forgave us all our trespasses, erasing the record that stood against us with its legal demands. He set this aside, nailing it to the cross. He disarmed the rulers and authorities and made a public example of them, triumphing over them in it. (Colossians 2:13-15)

As I write, the Winter Olympics has just recently been on our screens. My eldest daughter really enjoys watching sport and she was intrigued by all the new and sometimes rather strange disciplines one gets to experience at these games.

As part of her 'education' I thought it would be fun for the family to watch a famous movie that came out when I was younger. It was based on a true story and is about a bobsled team from Jamaica who battle against the odds to compete at the Calgary Winter Olympics in 1988.

One of the recurring jokes that runs throughout the film is

whenever the team crashes, someone shouts out from the tangled wreck and asks if everyone is still alive.

I want to ask the same question today – are you alive?

We need to understand that sin causes spiritual death. Death that does not begin when our spirit leaves our bodies when we breathe our last, but a death that has already begun.

Paul explains here that without choosing to follow Jesus, without us choosing to sacrifice our desires to prioritise Jesus' desires in our lives, without us putting off the old self and embracing the new self, found only in Him – without Jesus our spirits are dead.

This spiritual death for the whole of humanity began in The Beginning when the first human beings decided to disobey God and thereby allowed sin and death to enter all of creation as well as breaking our relationship and connection with God. This sadly means we are born into a fallen and broken creation. We start life with a dead spirit and a broken God-relationship.

But we can be made alive again in Christ!

When we decide to follow Jesus and choose to live life His way, the penalty for our sin (death) has already been paid through Jesus' sacrifice on the cross, as we learned yesterday. When we accept Jesus and turn to Him, the dead spirit within us is made alive. We are born-again because new life has entered us. We experience a birth in the spirit in addition to our physical birth. We become alive in Christ and our connection and relationship with God is restored through Christ.

The only way to eternal life is through Jesus because Jesus is the only one who paid the penalty for our sin on our behalf. Eternal life is His gift to give, and His alone.

This eternal life is not something reserved for one fine day when 'I'm up in heaven somewhere'. No. It is the very life that Jesus breathes into us to enliven our spirits when we choose to follow Him today.

Eternal life starts now in Christ and continues beyond physical death. It extends into eternity where we will all one day become physically alive again as well – re-created bodies and born again spirits joined together, living in the presence of God on the new earth and the new heaven forever.

So, I ask the question again – are you alive?

I pray that if you are alive in Christ, you will continue to live close to Jesus. And if you are not, that you will feel the gentle nudging of the Holy Spirit who is calling you by name and inviting you to come alive today.

Jesus, thank you that you have called me by name. That you have invited me to enter this amazing relationship with you. Thank you that as I choose to follow you today, and every day, that you enliven my spirit. Thank you that I am a new creation, that I am born again, with a new and living spirit within me.

Amen.

DAY 38 – THE WAY OF LOVE

Therefore be imitators of God, as beloved children, and live in love, as Christ loved us and gave himself up for us, a fragrant offering and sacrifice to God. (Ephesians 5:1-2)

'Follow the leader' was a playground game I enjoyed when I was a child. One person was chosen to be the leader, and then everyone else had to copy and imitate everything the leader did, usually whilst walking around the playground in a single file line.

As followers of Jesus, we are called to do just that – to follow His lead.

Indeed, Jesus was also following the leader when he was on earth. "'Very truly, I tell you, the Son can do nothing on his own, but only what he sees the Father doing; for whatever the Father does, the Son does likewise." (John 5:19).

Jesus listened to God the Father and responded to Him.

In the same way, through the Holy Spirit, we need to be communicating with Jesus and responding to his leading today.

The passage we are looking at now comes at the end of a longer section of Paul's letter to the Christians in Ephesus. He has just given several instructions on how one should be living if they are indeed following Christ.

He encourages them, and us, to avoid sensuality and indulging in impurity, not to be greedy or self-seeking. We should not lie, steal, use unwholesome language, be full or anger, rage, slander or bitterness. We should not get into fights. But rather, we must renew our minds, speak truthfully, try to resolve issues that make us angry, be encouraging with our words to help build others up. We should endeavour to be kind, compassionate and forgiving. In short, we are called to live a life of love.

As we live a life of love, Paul encourages us that we are indeed following the leader – Jesus, as this is how He lived.

It was His love for us that led Him to the cross. Jesus knowingly and willingly gave Himself to die on the cross in our place – the final and eternal sacrifice that only He could be, to pay the price for our sinfulness.

We are told that His sacrifice was a 'fragrant offering'. This means that it was acceptable. It was sufficient to pay the debt.

Jesus loved us to the point of death.

Living as Jesus lived means loving others even if it takes us to the point of death too.

It is not an easy or comfortable calling.

These days I hear a lot about 'toxic people'. We are told to love others, but if they are 'toxic' and are causing our mental health to suffer as a result, we should cut them out of our lives.

Jesus loved toxic people. He embraced them and their toxicity. In fact, he took their toxic nature upon himself and died for them so that they might live free from it.

We are also called to love people we may find 'toxic'.

Now hear what I am saying here. We need to be careful when we are dealing with broken and hurting people, for their sake as well as for our own. We don't need to allow ourselves to get sucked into their destructive behavioural patterns or wrong ways of thinking, but we are called to love them.

Sometimes saying 'no' is the most loving thing we can do for a person, even if they can't see it as love at the time. Yet sometimes saying 'yes' is the most loving thing to do. So how do we know what course of action is the best in a particular situation?

We need to be following the leader while we live lives of love. Jesus knows that person better than we do. The best strategy is to simply follow His leading.

By keeping in step with the Holy Spirit, we can live the lives of sacrificial love that Jesus calls us to live.

Jesus, help me to live a life of love. As I look to you for help and direction, help me to love those around me as you would have me love them.
Amen.

DAY 39 – CONTINUE

And you who were once estranged and hostile in mind, doing evil deeds, he has now reconciled in his fleshly body through death, so as to present you holy and blameless and irreproachable before him—provided that you continue securely established and steadfast in the faith, without shifting from the hope promised by the gospel (Colossians 1:21-23)

I am blessed to be the father of three children.

Becoming a biological father is rather easy. I won't go into the details here, but let's just say, if the two people concerned are both fertile, babies happen.

However, remaining a father is difficult. Every day I need to care for and provide for my children. It is something I have dedicated myself to for a long time. I get the joy of seeing them grow and develop. I have the privilege of building relationships with them, of teaching them and helping them as they grow. I am loved and I love to love them in return.

Becoming a father is easy, but remaining a father takes a lifetime of hard work and dedication.

We can see some parallels here with the Christian life too. There comes a point of decision on the journey of faith where someone decides to either believe in and follow Jesus, or not. It could have taken a long while for the person to reach this decision, but the making of it is relatively straight forward – either you believe, or you do not.

But the point of decision, or the 'day of salvation' as some may call it, is not an end in itself. It is just the beginning.

It is a mistake to think that because I decided to follow Jesus or said a 'special' prayer the deal is done and finished with – and that I can now return to life as normal.

No.

Jesus transforms our lives.

If we truly have Jesus living within us and working in our lives, He will change things and you will begin to change because your old self cannot co-exist with the new.

We were once enemies of God but are now adopted into His family. Things *will* change.

At salvation our spirits are made alive and are completely renewed within us (see Day 37). So, we *are* saved.

After that point, our minds need renewing. Our behaviours and attitudes begin to change, slowly growing to be more like Jesus. We need to continue in Christ. This is not instantaneous; it is a process. So, we *are being* saved.

I think the image of a spiral to help us understand our discipleship – the slow and gradual process of becoming more like Jesus – a helpful one. The centre of the spiral represents becoming completely mature in Christ, which as we have already said will only fully happen in eternity. The outer edge represents the starting point when we first decide to follow Jesus. Through our discipleship journey, we move both towards the centre and sometimes we move outwards again for a bit. We learn, we grow, we change our ideas, we behave differently. Gradually we move around the spiral towards the centre. We may revisit some of the same issues again and again along our journey as we go round the spiral, but each time is an opportunity to take a step towards Jesus or further away from Him. So, salvation is also a process.

One day our present bodies will die. Our spirits that are made alive will continue to live and one day we will be given recreated new bodies to live forever with Jesus on the new earth and the new heaven. This will be the ultimate fulfilment of God's salvation plan. A complete and total restoration of our relationship with Him in body, spirit, and mind. So, we *shall* be saved.

We should not take salvation for granted.

Paul urges the Colossian Christians to continue in the faith. Faith needs to be worked on every day.

I would encourage us to do the same – continue in the faith. Continue to grow in relationship with Jesus. Continue to pray. Continue to worship together, building and encouraging each other in the faith. Continue to learn more about God. Continue to become more mature in Christ, day by day. Continue to hold fast to the hope of the gospel. Keep going.

Jesus, help me to continue in the faith. May I become more and more like you. Change me. I don't want to be the same person. I choose to take off my old self and put on the new that only you can offer. Help me to endure. To run this race of faith without giving up.
Amen.

DAY 40 – RAISED WITH CHRIST

So if you have been raised with Christ, seek the things that are above, where Christ is, seated at the right hand of God. Set your minds on things that are above, not on things that are on earth, for you have died, and your life is hidden with Christ in God. When Christ who is your life is revealed, then you also will be revealed with him in glory. (Colossians 3:1-4)

Easter eggs – you either love them or you hate them.

I must admit I have a love-hate relationship with them. I like chocolate, so that is something in their favour. However, I don't like the way chocolate and cute bunnies distract people from the amazing reason for our celebrations – that Jesus is ALIVE!

When I became a Christian in my teenage years, I still liked receiving Easter eggs (and I still do). However, they took on a deeper significance for me.

Looking at the outside of the chocolate egg, you often see markings that look a bit like rocks. For me, the hollow egg represented the tomb where Jesus' body was buried. As I broke the egg open, it was with delight that I discovered, along with the women who visited the tomb early on Easter morning, that the tomb was empty. Jesus was not there. He had risen.

Easter Sunday is the most significant celebration of the Christian faith. Without the resurrection, there would be no point to Christianity at all.

Easter Sunday is a joyful celebration. We remember how Jesus, having died for us, also rose again for us.

Death is defeated and eternal life is promised.

In His resurrection we see God's salvation plan unveiled for the world to see – that we are invited to be part of.

We see Jesus confirming beyond doubt that He is who He said He was – The Son of God.

We see the ultimate victory of good over evil.

We see Jesus' resurrection reflected in our own journey of faith. He was dead but has been raised again to new life. Just as we were once dead in our sins, our spirits have been made newly alive within us as we believe in Jesus and choose to follow Him. We are born again.

We identify with Jesus' death, burial, and resurrection through water baptism. We die to our old self, as we go under, into a watery grave, and rise out of the water into new life.

We also look ahead to a time that is still to come. Where physical resurrection will happen for us too. The day when we will be raised with Christ and be given recreated physical bodies (Philippians 3:21). Those who believe in Jesus and have continued in the faith will live and reign with Christ forever on a new heaven and a new earth (Revelation 21:1).

This Easter, let us take Paul's advice and set our hearts on things above. And as we do, we will begin to see things from the perspective of eternity. The earthly things that seem so big and problematic will be shifted into their correct perspective – where Jesus is seated on the throne at God's right hand with all authority and power in the universe and beyond. Where we stand in a position of victory because we stand, hidden in Christ, and He is the ultimate victor.

Let us set our hearts on Jesus this Easter.

Jesus, I choose to set my heart on you this Easter. Help me to see the problems and circumstances I find myself in from your perspective. I look forward to the day when I am raised again with you for eternity – I celebrate you this Easter.
Amen.

FURTHER READING &
QUESTIONS 7

COLOSSIANS 3-4

Wider Reading – He is Alive

Jesus is the Resurrection - John 11:23-27

New Birth and Living Hope - 1 Peter 1:3

He is Risen - Luke 24:6-7

He is not Here - Matthew 28:5-6

Death has no Power - Romans 6:8-11

We Too Shall be Raised - 1 Corinthians 6:14

The First and the Last - Revelation 1:17-18

Discussion Questions – He is Alive

How does it make you feel, knowing that Jesus *had* to die?

What does living a life of love look like for you? How might this work out practically in your context?

Do you think saying 'no' to someone could be the most loving response in certain circumstances? How hard do you find it to say 'no' to someone?

How important is it for us to 'continue' on in our faith, rather than just relying upon a nice experience that happened once a long time ago?

What things do you do over the Easter period to help you remember Jesus' death and resurrection?

This chapter has focussed quite a lot on salvation and the forgiveness of sins offered to us by Jesus because of his death on the cross. If you are not saved, would you like to be? If you want to give your life to Jesus, speak to a Christian friend who can help you get started on the right path.

ABOUT THE AUTHOR

Matt McChlery is an author, songwriter, podcaster and church leader. He has won awards for his music and blogs.

Diagnosed with cancer in 2016, which he wrote about in his book 'Standing in the Storm: Living with Faith and Cancer' (Instant Apostle 2022), Matt is now in remission and has a passion to make every moment count for God's Kingdom.

Originally from Zimbabwe, Matt now lives with his wife, Verity and their three children in the United Kingdom.

OTHER BOOKS BY MATT MCCHLERY

Songcraft: Exploring the Art of Christian Songwriting

All Things New: Stories of Transformed Lives

Standing in the Storm: Living with Faith and Cancer

NOTES

DAY 2 – FROM SLAVE TO BROTHER

1. Based on the Introduction to Philemon in the NIV Zondervan Study Bible (Anglicised Version) © 2017, Hodder & Stoughton, pg 2484.

DAY 5 – GOD'S PLAN

1. Based on the notes in the NIV Zondervan Study Bible (Anglicised Version) © 2017, Hodder & Stoughton, Ephesians 1:7-10 pg 2400.

DAY 9 – MAKE EVERY EFFORT

1. Based on The Message of Ephesians: God's new society, John Stott © 1979 Inter-Varsity Press, pg 148.
2. Based on the notes in the NIV Zondervan Study Bible (Anglicised Version) © 2017, Hodder & Stoughton. Ephesians 4:3 pg 2405.

DAY 11 – JESUS VICTORIOUS

1. Based on the article 'The war that did not end at 11am on 11 November' by Tara Finn (https://history.blog.gov.uk/2018/11/09/the-war-that-did-not-end-at-11am-on-11-november/) accessed on 20th December 2021.

DAY 14 – TRUTH & RIGHTEOUSNESS

1. Based on a video of the sermon 'The Belt of Truth' by Matt McChlery (https://www.youtube.com/watch?v=vTeMaxeno1k&list=PLe-Y9VDogIB9DWt6sn-k2AwGKU5nSRYG3D&index=5) accessed on 17th December 2021.
2. Based on a video of the sermon 'The Breastplate of Righteousness' by Fiona Butcher (https://www.youtube.com/watch?v=DYPHlolO-vc&list=PLeY9VDogIB9DWt6sn-k2AwGKU5nSRYG3D&index=4) accessed on 17th December 2021.

NOTES

DAY 15 – FAITH & THE GOSPEL

1. Based on a video of the sermon 'The Gospel of Peace' by Matt McChlery (https://www.youtube.com/watch?v=nRt3e7dZ2_Q&list=PLe-Y9VDogIB9DWt6sn-k2AwGKU5nSRYG3D&index=3) accessed on 20th December 2021.

DAY 16 – SALVATION & THE WORD OF GOD

1. Based on a video of the sermon 'The Helmet of Salvation' by Mike Forrest (https://www.youtube.com/watch?v=8r-Hz6m5LpA&list=PLe-Y9VDogIB9DWt6sn-k2AwGKU5nSRYG3D&index=2) accessed on 22nd December 2021.
2. Based on a video of the sermon 'The Sword of the Spirit' by Keith Smith (https://www.youtube.com/watch?v=uhhAxA_Z7ZU&list=PLe-Y9VDogIB9DWt6sn-k2AwGKU5nSRYG3D&index=1) accessed on 22nd December 2021.

DAY 24 – BE HUMBLE

1. Based on the notes in the NIV Zondervan Study Bible © 2015 Zondervan, Philippians 2:5, page 2417.

DAY 28 – LIVE FOR JESUS

1. Based on Pollock, John (1977), p. 38 Wilberforce, New York: St. Martin's Press, ISBN 978-0-09-460780-4, OCLC 3738175

DAY 29 – PAUL IN CHAINS

1. Information found at https://www.history.com/this-day-in-history/nelson-mandela-released-from-prison accessed on 4th March 2022.

DAY 34 - THE PERSECUTED CHURCH

1. Statistics found on the Open Doors Website https://www.opendoorsuk.org/ accessed 13th May 2022.

DAY 35 – DEATH ON A CROSS

1. All forgiveness is found in Jesus. This includes those in the Old Testament as Jesus fulfilled the sacrificial system through His death. See Hebrews 10:1-18 which applies retrospectively as well as into the future.

DAY 36 – REDEMPTION AND FORGIVENESS

1. Based on a definition found at https://www.investopedia.com/terms/r/redemption.asp#:~:text=In%20finance%2C%20redemption%20describes%20the,shares%20from%20their%20fund%20manager accessed 22nd March 2022.